IBM Lotus Sametime 8 Essentials

A User's Guide

Mastering Online Enterprise Communication with this collaborative software

Marie L. Scott

Thomas Duff

BIRMINGHAM - MUMBAI

IBM Lotus Sametime 8 Essentials
A User's Guide

First published: September 2010

Production Reference: 1170910

Published by Packt Publishing Ltd.
32 Lincoln Road
Olton
Birmingham, B27 6PA, UK.

ISBN 978-1-849680-60-8

www.packtpub.com

Cover Image by Leisha Bryant (leishabryant@gmail.com)

Credits

Authors
Marie L. Scott
Thomas Duff

Reviewers
Luis Guirigay
Sjaak Ursinus
Rainier Varilla

Acquisition Editor
Rashmi Phadnis

Development Editor
Dhiraj Chandiramani

Technical Editor
Arun Nadar

Indexer
Monica Ajmera Mehta

Editorial Team Leader
Akshara Aware

Project Team Leader
Lata Basantani

Project Coordinator
Srimoyee Ghoshal

Proofreader
Kevin McGowan

Production Coordinator
Shantanu Zagade

Cover Work
Shantanu Zagade

About the Authors

Marie Scott is the Director of E-mail Services at Virginia Commonwealth University in Richmond, Virginia. Marie has a bachelor's degree in biology from James Madison University and a certificate in Information Systems from Virginia Commonwealth University. She has had dual advanced certification in Notes/Domino administration and development since version 4.0. Marie began working with Lotus Notes in 1996, and has worked in networking, systems integration, and e-mail systems since 1987. Her primary interest is in Domino administration in complex environments. She has managed large e-mail migration projects and recently completed a project to transition university students to cloud computing. Marie has been a speaker at conferences including Lotusphere featuring IBM/Lotus technologies. Marie can be contacted at `http://crashtestchix.com`.

I'd like to thank the following individuals without whom this book would not have been possible:

To Tom Duff—simply the best co-author—thanks for knowing when to let me drive, when to let me rant, and when to make sure we were both laughing. I'm ready to write another book any time, just say the word!

To my friends and colleagues: Connie Whetstine, Joni Snyder, Josie Barbie, Pam McGhee, Diane Talley, Linda Hairfield, Scott Davis, Mark Willis, Tonie Ellerson, James Henderson, Bruce Batchelder, Jason Fortney, Russell Pociluyko, Joe Lichtenstein, Judi Hoover Born, Julia Whetstone, Amy Blumenfield, Kathy Brown, Susan Bulloch, Gabriella Davis, Kitty Elsmore, Eileen Fitzgerald, Maureen Leland, Kathleen McGivney, Mary Beth Raven, Jess Stratton, Francie Tanner, Steve Katz, Carolyn Bourdow, Nelda, and Buz Snyder—thank you for your encouragement and support.

And finally to my family—my parents, sister and brothers: my thanks and love for always being there.

Thomas Duff (also known as "Duffbert") is a software developer focusing on Lotus collaboration technologies in Portland, Oregon. He started working with Lotus Notes in 1996 in version R3 and has written and maintained hundreds of applications in large enterprises through the years. He also holds Lotus principal development certifications starting at version 4 and going up to version 8 as well as Microsoft and Java certifications. Tom is a prolific writer, both in industry publications and at his website, Duffbert's Random Musings, at http://www.duffbert.com. He also is a frequent speaker at conferences and events focusing on Lotus technologies.

I always maintained I'd never write a technical book due to the time and effort it takes. Yet when Marie approached me with this opportunity, I felt as if most of the writing I've done over the years was leading exactly to this point in time. I can't think of anyone who would make a better co-author, as well as someone who would still be speaking to me when we finished. Thanks for pushing me out of my comfort zone, Marie.

A special thanks to Libby Ingrassia, my first editor. Had you not taken a chance on my writing an article as an unknown author, my part of this book might not have happened.

For Susan, Ian, and Cam, thanks for the care and feeding of the author. Now that the book is finished, I promise to get out of the basement more and to get my vitamin D levels back up to the minimum recommended level... really!

Acknowledgement

It's been said that it takes a village to raise a child. It's also true that it takes a community to write a book. Given that IBM/Lotus software is centered on collaboration, it isn't surprising that we relied heavily on the collaboration of many in our professional and personal community to make this book as thorough as possible.

Thank you to the team at Packt Publishing for their invaluable assistance and for giving us the opportunity to become first time authors. Also many thanks go to Esther Schindler, Rich Santalesa, and the rest of the members of the Internet Press Guild. Their group experience, along with the unselfish sharing of their knowledge, helped us avoid a number of pitfalls, and start the journey to print.

This book would have been next to impossible without the assistance of Gabriella and Tim Davis and the team at The Turtle Partnership. They graciously provided us with access to a test server environment. Thanks also to the Bleedyellow and Lotus Greenhouse sites which were invaluable in the creation of the chapters on Sametime Advanced and Sametime 8.5 and 8.5.1. Special recognition goes to Mary Beth Raven and Tracee Wolf as well for making sure we had the contacts and materials we needed. We received valuable feedback and input on our writing and ideas from various individuals over the course of the months it took to put our words onto the page, including Susan Bulloch, Paul Mooney, Wes Morgan, Gabriella Davis, Kathy Brown, Chris Miller, Carl Tyler, and Steve McDonagh.

Many thanks also go to our colleagues who stepped in at the end of the project to provide technical editing within a very short timeframe: Bob Balaban, Casey Brown, Susan Bulloch, Sean Burgess, Mitch Cohen, Corey Davis, Gabriella Davis, Gregg Eldred, Steve McDonagh, Stuart McIntyre, Chris Miller, Paul Mooney, and Julian Robichaux.

As co-authors, who for most of the project were three thousand miles apart, we may not have been quite so organized and on schedule without the use of Dropbox. It's software that just works.

Finally to our families, friends, fellow bloggers, tweeters, chat partners, and Facebook friends — we thank you for your encouragement and enthusiasm for this project. When things started to drag and we wondered where the next few pages were going to come from, you were there to remind us to keep laughing and keep going!

About the Reviewers

Luis Guirigay is a Senior IT Specialist at PSC Group, LLC (http://www.psclistens.com) where he specializes in Administration, High Level Support, Performance Tuning, and advanced deployments. He is also a Lotus Evangelist and a Developer who loves to write code every time he gets a chance. He has been working with IBM Lotus products for more than 12 years and is an IBM Certified Administrator for Domino 5,6,7,8, and 8.5; Sametime 7.5, 8, and 8.5; Lotus Connections 2 and 2.5 and Websphere Portal 6.0 and 6.1 and an IBM Certified Developer in Domino 5,6,7,8, and 8.5 and Lotus Workflow. He also has experience with WebSphere Application Server, DB2, Tivoli, and ILWWCM. Luis has published multiple IBM Redbooks related to Domino, Workplace, DB2, and System i. He can be reached at lguirigay@psclistens.com.

Thanks to my wife Mariu, my son Adrian, and my mom Nancy for all your love and support.

Rainier Varilla has been the technical lead on many software opportunities at large and small accounts as a Collaboration Specialist. Rainier Varilla has been engaged on numerous customer engagements, where he delivered technical presentations, Proof-of-Concepts (POC) or Proof-of-Technology (POT) sessions and demonstrated IBM software solutions such as WebSphere Portal Server (WPS), IBM Lotus Web Content Management (ILWCM), Lotus Connections, Lotus Notes, Lotus Sametime, and Lotus Live. While working on these opportunities, Rainier Varilla developed contacts with the customer's business and IT leaders in order to gain insight into their business needs and pains, as well as to obtain a thorough understanding of their technical environment. Rainier Varilla also worked closely with individual contributors at customer sites to make recommendations, resolve open issues, and escalate through the customer management chain to demonstrate business need and solution alternatives.

I would like to thank my colleagues at IBM for validating my reviews to the book, as well as my family and friends for supporting me in reviewing this book. Lastly, I would like to thank IBM and my customers for affording me the opportunity to work for them and gain valuable experiences which I was able to use in reviewing this book.

Table of Contents

Preface

IBM Lotus Sametime software allows you to collaborate and communicate with others in real time. By using Sametime, you can communicate with your peers and teammates with the Sametime Connect client, embedded Sametime integration with Lotus Notes, or Microsoft Outlook e-mail, or on mobile devices like a Blackberry. You can connect with your colleagues through text, voice, video, or by setting up an online meeting with colleagues in several sites or countries. You get the information you need to do your job and make better and faster decisions.

This user guide enables you, no matter what your skill level, to develop and increase your knowledge of Sametime and helps you learn how to use each feature from start to finish. It shows how you can effectively collaborate with your colleagues and teammates both in your organization and outside your organization by using the features of Sametime. It's practical, direct, and most of all, fun!

This book takes you from the basics of Sametime through to the most advanced features with a focus on real work-related situations along with plenty of screen prints to guide you. You'll learn everything from how to conduct a quick chat to conducting an online meeting. Perhaps you want to learn how to take advantage of Sametime's telephony features or set up an online poll. The book starts by teaching you how to install Sametime and set up a contact list of people with whom you interact. Next, you learn how the chat feature of Sametime works, from using basic text to sharing screen-capture images. You learn how to use Sametime both within an organization and with other external instant messaging services like AOL, Yahoo, and Google. However, Sametime isn't restricted to just the Sametime client. You learn how to use Sametime from a web browser as well as from a mobile device. Find out how to use meeting rooms with screen sharing, whiteboarding, audio and video features, as well as how Sametime integrates into an organization's phone system so that you have a single place to go for all your communication and collaboration needs. Learn how Sametime Advanced features like persistent chats and broadcast communities can help your project teams stay organized. Finally, you learn about the new features included with Sametime 8.5 and 8.5.1.

Dive into Sametime and learn to use all the features of this rich collaboration software tool.

Who this book is for

If you want to learn how to use IBM Lotus Sametime, then this book is for you. No matter if you're new to Sametime or a Sametime power user, this book contains something for you. The focus is on using Sametime as a user and does not include information about development or administration of a Sametime environment. Any user of Sametime in an organization will be able to take this book, sit down at their computer, and learn how to use each feature of Sametime from start to finish.

What this book covers

Chapter 1, At the Starting Line: Know Your Sametime Client talks about the different types of Sametime clients and why Sametime instant messaging is a good choice for you and your organization.

Chapter 2, Getting Connected: Configuring and Using Sametime for Lotus Notes is a chapter where you'll learn about the Embedded Sametime client within Lotus Notes. Included is what you'll need to know about logging into Sametime, configuring the client for your particular style of work, and how to begin chatting with others in your Sametime community.

Chapter 3, Getting Connected: Configuring and Using Sametime Connect covers the installation of Sametime Connect client onto your Windows, Mac, or Linux operating system with step-by-step instructions. Learn about configuring the client for your particular style of work, and how to install Sametime plug-ins to customize your Sametime Connect client.

Chapter 4, Managing Your Connections: Making the most of your Sametime Contacts is a chapter where you'll learn how to create and organize your Sametime contact list. Find out how you can create chats with three or more people and manage your presence awareness to let people know your current status.

Chapter 5, Power Chatting: Making the most of Sametime Instant Messaging is a chapter where you'll start using advanced chat features such as rich text, attachments, emoticons, graphics, and screen captures, as well as adding voice and video into your chats.

Chapter 6, Spread the Word: Connecting to other Messaging Communities is a chapter where you'll learn how to connect to both local and external Sametime communities. Discover how you can connect with external third-party messaging providers like Yahoo, AOL, and Google. You also learn the difference between Domino and LDAP authentication.

Chapter 7, iNotes and Sametime – Chatting from the Web speaks about using Sametime from within the Lotus iNotes browser client. Discover how easy it is to chat with your contacts, add new contacts, and manage your presence awareness.

Chapter 8, Going Mobile – Installing and Using the Sametime Mobile Client helps you determine the type of mobile Sametime client you need and how to install Sametime on your mobile device. Become skilled at configuring Sametime Mobile, managing your contacts, and chatting with other Sametime users using your mobile device.

Chapter 9, Meeting Basics – Using Sametime to Create Virtual Meeting Spaces introduces you to Sametime Meeting Center, learning how to login, schedule and attend meetings, and save meetings for later playback. Find out how to add slides and files to the meeting, conduct instant polls, and have group chats while in the main meeting.

Chapter 10, Meeting Beyond the Conference Room – Using Additional Sametime Meeting Features shows you how to use Sametime Meeting Center to share your screen with others as well as collaborate on documents using the whiteboard feature. Add video and voice features to your meeting as well as optimize your settings to get the best performance possible.

Chapter 11, Take Your Instant Messaging to the Next level – Sametime Advanced will teach us to use Sametime Advanced to go beyond the core features of Sametime and become skilled at using its features like broadcast communities, persistent chats, skill taps, instant polls, and Announcements.

Chapter 12, Speak Up – Taking Advantage of Sametime Unified Telephony is a chapter where you'll find out how Sametime Unified Telephony can be used in your company or organization from the Sametime client to route calls to various devices, make and answer calls online, and schedule conference calls instantly.

Appendix A, Sametime 8.5 and 8.5.1 New Features talks about the new features of Sametime that will be available in versions 8.5 and 8.5.1, such as the browser-based chat client and the Apple iPhone Sametime client.

Appendix B, Using Sametime in Chat-Enabled Applications shows how Sametime integrates chat features into other applications such as Lotus Notes, Lotus Quickr, Lotus Connections, Microsoft Outlook, Microsoft Office, and Microsoft SharePoint.

Appendix C, Additional Sametime Resources lists a variety of different resources you can use to go beyond the scope of this book to discover even more about Sametime and its various features and benefits.

What you need for this book

This book assumes you are using Lotus Sametime version 8.0.2.

Conventions

In this book, you will find a number of styles of text that distinguish between different kinds of information. Here are some examples of these styles, and an explanation of their meaning.

Code words in text are shown as follows: "In most cases the plug-ins are packaged in a `.jar` format and are added as you would with any other Sametime plug-in."

New terms and **important words** are shown in bold. Words that you see on the screen, in menus or dialog boxes for example, appear in the text like this: "clicking the **Next** button moves you to the next screen".

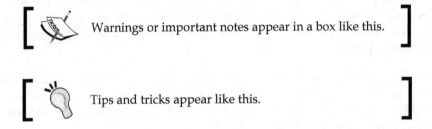

Warnings or important notes appear in a box like this.

Tips and tricks appear like this.

Reader feedback

Feedback from our readers is always welcome. Let us know what you think about this book—what you liked or may have disliked. Reader feedback is important for us to develop titles that you really get the most out of.

To send us general feedback, simply send an e-mail to feedback@packtpub.com, and mention the book title via the subject of your message.

If there is a book that you need and would like to see us publish, please send us a note in the **SUGGEST A TITLE** form on www.packtpub.com or e-mail suggest@packtpub.com.

If there is a topic that you have expertise in and you are interested in either writing or contributing to a book, see our author guide on www.packtpub.com/authors.

Errata

Although we have taken every care to ensure the accuracy of our content, mistakes do happen. If you find a mistake in one of our books—maybe a mistake in the text or the code—we would be grateful if you would report this to us. By doing so, you can save other readers from frustration and help us improve subsequent versions of this book. If you find any errata, please report them by visiting http://www.packtpub.com/support, selecting your book, clicking on the **errata submission form** link, and entering the details of your errata. Once your errata are verified, your submission will be accepted and the errata will be uploaded on our website, or added to any list of existing errata, under the Errata section of that title. Any existing errata can be viewed by selecting your title from http://www.packtpub.com/support.

Piracy

Piracy of copyright material on the Internet is an ongoing problem across all media. At Packt, we take the protection of our copyright and licenses very seriously. If you come across any illegal copies of our works, in any form, on the Internet, please provide us with the location address or website name immediately so that we can pursue a remedy.

Please contact us at copyright@packtpub.com with a link to the suspected pirated material.

We appreciate your help in protecting our authors, and our ability to bring you valuable content.

Questions

You can contact us at questions@packtpub.com if you are having a problem with any aspect of the book, and we will do our best to address it.

1
At the Starting Line: Know Your Sametime Client

You've heard about instant messaging. You've heard about e-mail. You've probably also heard about online meetings. So how might these three forms of communication be connected and what does this have to do with you? If you're reading this book you're about to find out.

You're at the starting line. Imagine that you have a new job and today is your first day. You turn on your computer and start looking for your e-mail program. Along the way, you see a program called IBM Lotus Sametime. What's that, you might ask. Is it something I need? Will it help me to do my job better?

Sametime is a software package for instant messaging and web conferencing. It allows you to have instant conversations or "chat" with your co-workers, have online meetings, share files, and much more. In this book, we will show you everything you need to know to use Sametime and get the most value possible from all of its many features. By the time you finish reading, not only will you be a Sametime "power user", but you'll wonder how you were able to get along without it.

In this chapter, you'll learn the following:

- Why instant messaging is important
- Why Sametime is an excellent choice for enterprise instant messaging
- The different types of Sametime clients
- The different versions of Sametime, along with the significant features of each

What's all the fuss about instant messaging?

You may be saying to yourself, "I already have an instant messaging client". If you are familiar with instant messaging or IM for short, it's likely that you use one or more IM clients for personal purposes. Skype has IM and voice communications. Google has Google Chat and Google Voice. AOL has AIM, Microsoft has MSN Messenger, and Yahoo! has Yahoo! Instant Messenger. And let's not forget tools like Pidgin and Trillian that allow you to connect to multiple instant messaging systems all from one chat window.

But remember—you're at the office and many workplaces block personal chat services at the corporate firewall for security reasons. Exactly how might instant messaging work in an office environment? To give you a glimpse of instant messaging in action in the workplace, let's look at the following scenarios:

- You have a deadline for a report and you need one final detail from your teammate, Joan. You try to call Joan, but your call is transferred to voicemail. Minutes are ticking by. Wait—you notice that Joan is online in Sametime, so you "ping" her and she responds with the detail you need to complete the report!

- You're working on a helpdesk support line and you receive an incoming call. You don't have the necessary information to provide an answer to the user, but while the user is on the phone, you can IM your team through Sametime to see if any of the team members know the answer. And guess what—Bashir responds back in the chat window with the correct response!

- As a team manager you're responsible for making sure that progress is being made on an important project while you're away from the office at a conference. From your Blackberry, you can chat using Sametime Mobile to get a quick status report from Scott and Connie while you're waiting for your first session to begin!

- You need to set up a meeting, only to find out that two of the key meeting attendees, Chadna and Huan, will be at a remote office. You can still schedule the meeting using the Sametime Meeting Center; you can have an online meeting with slides, voice, and audio no matter where the attendees are located!

Why use Sametime?

Obviously Sametime is not the only instant messaging or web meeting software tool available. However, in the business world, there are other usability factors to consider when choosing an instant messaging or online meeting client. Can you guarantee that the person on the other end of the chat is who they say they are? Are you sure that the content you type to the other person is secure from others who might be monitoring your connection? Is the password you're using encrypted? Why would that be important? Let's say you're a stock broker communicating with another broker over IM about the value of a stock. Would it be appropriate for that chat conversation to not be secure or encrypted? Probably not! With Sametime, you can communicate with others knowing that you're protected from eavesdroppers and malicious third parties.

Also, managing organizational knowledge is as critically important as maintaining a secured conversation. Pharmaceutical, health care, military, and financial organizations also must comply with international, federal, and state regulations regarding securing and maintaining copies of electronic communication that includes instant messaging. For profit, companies can't afford to have company secrets made public because a chat conversation or online meeting wasn't secured.

We've mentioned the importance of communication, but what about integration? Does your communication client integrate with other software running in your organization, making it easy to connect and collaborate? Trying to integrate consumer IM clients and business-related software is a difficult and time-consuming task. But with Sametime, those concerns disappear. Not only do you have a secure method of communication, but you also have a client you can use from your e-mail system, the web, your phone, or in an online application. Sametime integrates with the Lotus family of software, as well as with Microsoft Office, Microsoft Outlook, and Microsoft SharePoint.

We haven't even touched on Sametime's other strength as an office tool — online meetings. How many times have you tried to set up a meeting only to find out that someone is traveling on the only day you can set up the meeting? Or you have many slides you want to display during the meeting, but want to be able to annotate them and have users comment during the process? What about user polls or the ability to add video or audio during an online meeting? And what if you need to share your desktop during this meeting and share its contents or display an application during the course of a meeting? Sametime allows you to do that. Sametime online meetings provide a secure web-driven environment for meetings in and out of the physical office environment. No matter if you're separated by time zone differences or are using different types of workstations such as PCs, Macs, or Linux, you can still log into to the meeting center to attend the online meeting. Need to schedule an online meeting every week? You can do that! Need to allow white boarding during the meeting for planning purposes? You can do that! You can open and schedule a meeting from your Sametime client. So while Sametime is about chatting, it's also about connecting with colleagues and teammates for work groups and discussions.

Types of Sametime clients

Another major benefit of Sametime is that it is not a "one-size-fits-most" offering. The Sametime client set allows instant messaging connections from various types of workstations and mobile devices. Sametime uses a central company directory for displaying contact information which can be customized—even including employee photos. Depending on the way you and your organization work, there are a number of different types of Sametime clients to best fit everyone's needs.

Sametime Embedded Client—the Sametime Embedded Client is what you use when you're running the Lotus Notes e-mail client and Sametime is "built in" to the client experience. In most cases, Sametime will be running in the Lotus Notes Sidebar as a "widget", or a mini-application within Lotus Notes. It can be set to automatically sign in when you start Lotus Notes, and you don't have to be concerned with running or starting a separate program for running Sametime.

Sametime Connect—Sametime Connect is the stand-alone Sametime client. When it is launched, it runs as a separate application, and is similar in nature to what you'd see if you were using an IM client like AIM or Skype. This configuration is ideal for users who don't often use the Notes client but need to have the capabilities of Sametime available on a constant basis.

Sametime Mobile—Sametime Mobile allows you to use Lotus Sametime instant messaging on Research in Motion BlackBerry devices, Microsoft Windows Mobile devices, Sony Ericsson mobile devices, and Nokia ESeries devices. The Sametime Mobile client is downloaded to the device and provides basic chat and "awareness" so you can remain in contact while away from your office computer.

Sametime for Lotus iNotes—Sametime basic functionality is also available to Lotus iNotes users. Lotus iNotes is the web collaboration client for e-mail and calendaring available for Lotus Notes users.

The Sametime system offerings

Why use one Sametime client versus another? The availability of Sametime clients and features may depend on how your computer is configured and which version of the Sametime server is in use at your company. There are a number of features that you may or may not have available based on the level of Sametime software installed in your workplace. There are four levels of Sametime available: Entry, Standard, Advanced, and Unified Telephony. Each subsequent level adds features to the previous level and determines what options you will have at your disposal.

Sametime Entry—Sametime Entry is the "get your feet wet" version of Sametime. As its name suggests, it provides a basic set of options which include instant messaging, online awareness, file sharing, geographic information, screen capture, and Microsoft product integration.

Sametime Standard—Sametime Standard builds on the Sametime Entry features to include web conferencing with video and/or audio, as well as instant screen sharing; Voice over IP (VoIP) chat for those installations on a VoIP network, support for Sametime Mobile, and integration with public IM systems like AOL, Google, and Yahoo through the Sametime Gateway system. Some integrated telephony voice options are available with third party vendor support like "click to call" and call management.

Sametime Advanced—Sametime Advanced is the next tier. It includes all the features of Sametime Entry and Sametime Standard plus expanded chat and web conference functions. Sametime Advanced offers chat room service, broadcast chat messages, and screen sharing from within a web conference.

Sametime Unified Telephony—Sametime Unified Telephony adds "unified communication" functionality. Many organizations are seeking to integrate chat, e-mail, and office applications, with what has typically been only phone-based functionality like voice mail, call routing, and caller presence. Sametime Unified Telephony adds those features to the Sametime product set.

Feature	Sametime Entry	Sametime Standard	Sametime Advanced	Sametime Unified Telephony
Instant messaging	•	•	•	
Presence awareness	•	•	•	
Persistent group chat			•	
Broadcast			•	
Instant screen sharing			•	

Feature	Sametime Entry	Sametime Standard	Sametime Advanced	Sametime Unified Telephony
Microsoft Office/Outlook integration	•	•	•	
Web conferencing		•	•	
VoIP chat		•	•	
Video		•	•	
Support for mobile devices		•	•	
Interoperability with supported public IM networks		•	•	
Softphone				•
Click to call/conference				•

Summary

After a brief introduction to the different Sametime clients and features, you now know how Sametime can improve your productivity and effectiveness on a daily basis. We've described some reasons why you and your company might be using Sametime. We've also described the different software levels and what options may be available.

2
Getting Connected: Configuring and Using Sametime for Lotus Notes

Samantha has recently upgraded to Lotus Notes 8.5.1. She received information regarding the upgrade that said she can now use Sametime instant messaging from her Notes workspace. What does that mean, where is it, and how does she start using it? If, like Samantha, you are a Lotus Notes version 8.x e-mail client user, the Sametime client can be included as a part of your e-mail installation.

In this chapter, you'll learn how to:

- Determine if you have the Sametime integrated client
- Login to Sametime
- Use single sign-on to simplify your Sametime login
- Gather the information you need to connect to Sametime
- Set up your friends and colleagues in your Sametime contact list
- Begin a chat in Sametime

So exactly what is the "embedded" Sametime client?

The "embedded" or integrated Sametime client is the version of Sametime that runs within the Lotus Notes client. Sametime can be built into the Notes client software install package, so you don't have to install additional software in order to use instant messaging. As soon as your Notes install is complete you've got e-mail and instant messaging!

How can you tell if your install included Sametime? If you're using Lotus Notes 8.0 or higher and if Sametime has been installed for your organization, Sametime will most likely appear as a toolbar option in the Lotus Notes sidebar. You may also see this referred to as the Sametime "widget". A widget is a piece of software that is designed to display information in the sidebar area of the Notes client.

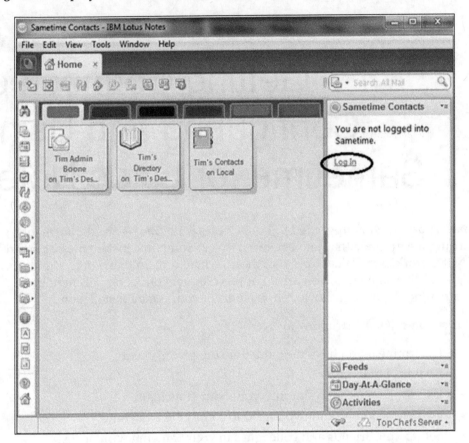

The embedded Sametime client expands and collapses in the sidebar as you click on **Sametime Contacts**. It is possible that you will only see the Sametime toolbar header without the **Log In** prompt. If that's the case, just click on the toolbar header and it will expand the widget so that it looks like the previous illustration. You may also find that the sidebar is very narrow and only shows icons. You can expand the sidebar by clicking on the divider between the sidebar and the Notes workspace, and dragging the divider to the width that is most convenient for you.

Getting connected to Sametime

Once you've confirmed that your Lotus Notes environment is enabled for Sametime, you'll discover that logging on is easy. You will see a **Log In** link on the Sametime widget, which you click in order to get the logon dialog box:

A few essential pieces of information are needed to complete this dialog box and they should be provided to you by your technical department, namely **Host server**, **User name**, and **Password**. The Host server field is the Sametime server name. As people connect to this server, you can see they are active and can chat with them. Your username is normally the same name or user id you use to sign on to your Lotus Notes client, but you may have a separate user id for Sametime depending on the type of authentication Sametime is using. Your password is most likely the same as your Notes client id password, but your technical department should provide you with this information.

If you want to automatically log into Sametime when you start up Lotus Notes, select the **Remember Password** and **Automatically log in** checkboxes. This combination ensures that you will always sign on to Sametime every time you are logged into Notes. And while this says "automatically", it's important to remember to keep your password up-to-date. The password in the dialog box will require an update for your login to Sametime to be successful.

Once you have completed the dialog box, click on **Log In**, and if your login information is correct, your Sametime client will show you connected to the server:

Starting Sametime with single sign-on

Jurgen also uses Lotus Notes and Sametime. However, when he starts Lotus Notes, he only needs to provide his Notes client password and he will be automatically connected to Sametime. How did he do that? Jurgen configured a Sametime user preference known as "single sign-on".

Each Sametime user is connected to a Sametime server. Your Sametime server is referred to as a "community" and each community has a unique name. When your Notes client is installed, your technical department may have configured it such that a default Sametime community has been set up for you. In the Sametime Community list it is very easy to determine as the word "default" is included as part of the server name. In some organizations or companies there may be multiple Sametime communities. Check with your Sametime administrator if you're not sure as to which community you should connect to.

Sametime has the ability to use Domino single sign-on. If your organization's Sametime community is configured such that your Sametime username is the same as your Notes client name, you can select the option to use Domino single sign-on. Single sign-on works by passing a secret key from Lotus Notes that identifies you to your Sametime server. Sametime will then recognize you as an authorized user and log you in without requiring a separate sign-on screen. Many organizations configure their Sametime server environment to allow this feature as it's simpler for you—the user! If you know this feature is available, you can click on the **Connectivity** button in the Sametime login dialog box and the options for your Sametime server connection will be displayed. Select the **Use Domino single sign-on if available** option and click on **OK** to save your choice.

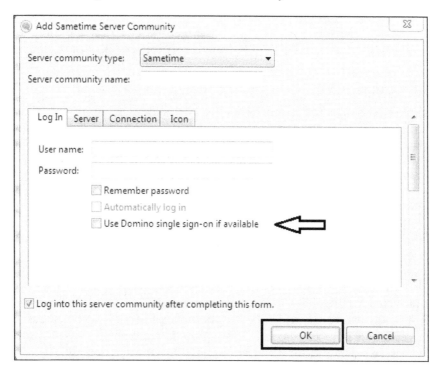

The next time you signin to Lotus Notes, you should see that your Sametime status already reflects that you're logged in and that you are available to chat.

Making Sametime work the best way for you

Sametime offers many features that allow you to create a collaborative chat environment that is easy-to-use and to manage. Because instant messaging can be used in so many different ways, Sametime includes options for you to modify individual user settings so that Sametime works best for you.

Here are some scenarios:

- Sharon is visually impaired and needs to modify software in order to communicate effectively with others.

- Because Mark's job requires it, he must maintain a copy of all his chat sessions. He wants to do this easily and control how it's done.

- Anisha doesn't want to always have to worry about changing her Sametime status automatically when she steps away from her workstation.

- Tania's boss likes to see words spelled correctly in all communication with her staff, even instant messaging. Tania would like to make sure spell checking is turned on for her Sametime chat windows.

You can customize Sametime to meet these requirements and more! To display the preference menu for the Sametime embedded client, you click on the down arrow on the right-side of your Sametime widget header. A drop-down menu will display with an option to view **Preferences**. Select **Preferences** as an option and you will now see the **Preferences** menu. Preferences can also be displayed from your Notes client by selecting **File | Preferences.** The options displayed are the same no matter how you access the menu.

To take this a step further, click on the Sametime entry and you'll see an expanded list of additional features. Many of these options don't require any changes, but you can make some selections to customize Sametime to work the way you want at any time. The **Preferences** window is shown in the following screenshot:

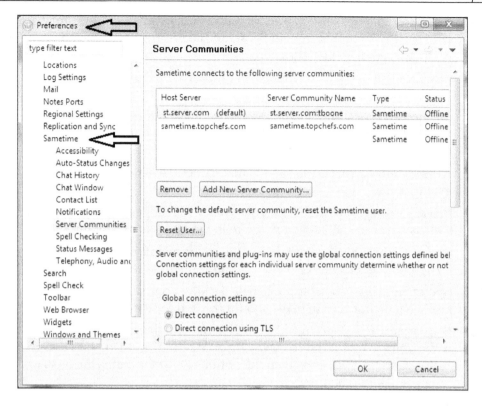

The following are the options:

- **Accessibility** - contains settings to make Sametime easier to use with screen readers for visually impaired users.

- **Auto-Status Changes** - controls the conditions under which Sametime will automatically change your status (**Available, Away, In A Meeting,** and **Do Not Disturb**) or log you off during periods of inactivity.

- **Chat History** - controls how Sametime will save your chat transcripts for you.

- **Chat Window** - controls how the Sametime chat window will appear, as well as font settings, time stamps, and how certain keystrokes are interpreted.

- **Contact List** - controls how Sametime will notify you during certain contact list activities, as well as how your contact list will be maintained and stored on the Sametime server.

- **Emoticon Palettes** - lists the active emoticons, or small graphic images to help convey emotions, in your Sametime client. You can also add or remove additional emoticon palettes here.

- **File Transfers** - controls where files transferred during a Sametime chat will be stored.

- **Geographic Location** - maintains geographical information about where you are as well as contact information about you. This information is displayed at the top of your Sametime profile and chats.

- **Notification** - controls the sounds that Sametime makes when certain events occur.

- **Privacy** - controls who can see you when you're logged onto Sametime, as well as who can contact you if you're in **Do Not Disturb** mode.

- **Server Communities** - contains all the technical information about how your Sametime client connects to one or more Sametime servers.

- **Spell Checking** - controls how spellchecking occurs in your Sametime client, and what dictionary language should be used for the spellchecking.

- **Status Messages** - specifies the basic status messages that are displayed when you are in **Available**, **Away**, **In A Meeting**, and **Do Not Disturb** mode. It also controls if you are given the option to edit the status message each time your status changes.

- **Telephony, Audio and Video** - controls the microphone, speaker, and video camera settings for your Sametime client if you have those available to use.

- **Web Conference Tools** - indicates what tools (microphone, speaker, and camera) you have available for web conferences.

Don't be overwhelmed by all the choices you have for configuring Sametime. As you become more of a Sametime expert, you'll know exactly what options you want or need to customize and streamline Sametime into your very own personalized instant messaging client.

Adding a contact

Now that you're logged into Sametime, you need to find someone to chat with. To add more people while you're working inside your contact list, right-click on the **Work** contact category. When you do that, a pop-up menu of options appear, one of which is **Add Contacts**. When you select that, you get a dialog box that allows you to enter all or part of a name of someone to add to your contact list:

Clicking on **Lookup** gives you a list of everyone that matches the name (or partial name) that you entered:

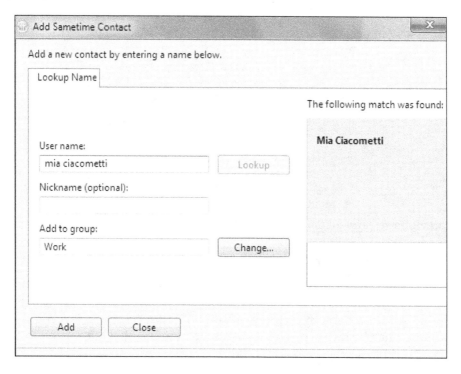

Clicking on **Add** adds the name you've selected to your contact list, and now the person appears on your screen every time you log into Sametime:

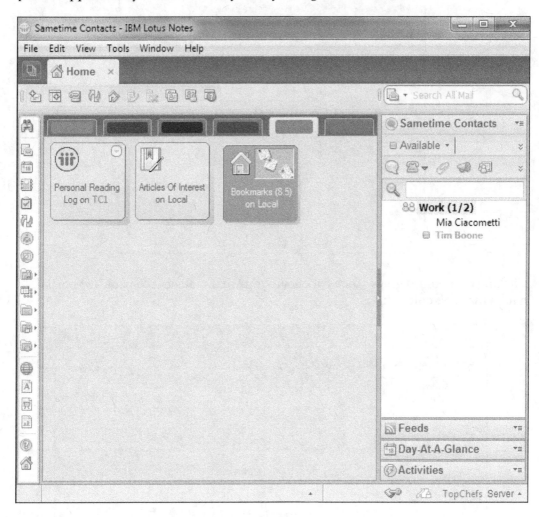

In the previous screenshot, since **Mia Ciacometti** is not showing up in green, we know she has not signed on and we can't send her a message at this time. But when she does sign on, we'll see her name turn green with a green icon next to it, and we can start a chat with her.

Another way to add contacts to your contact list is to select the person's name from the **Domino Address Book** in your organization. Right-click on their name and select **Add to Sametime Contact List**. This displays a dialog box that allows you to select or create a group to add the contact as well.

Your Notes **Inbox** can also be a source for adding Sametime contacts. You may notice that someone you interact with through e-mail has a green Sametime icon by their name. This indicates that they are a Sametime user too! Right-click on the sender's name and add them to the contact list from the dialog box, or easier yet—you can drag-and-drop their name into a group in your contact list. You'll find your contact list starts to look more like this:

What is Sametime "status"?

Sametime includes icons that provide information about a user's "status". Sametime status icons let you know when your contacts are available to chat, when they are in a meeting, or when they may be away from their desk. The icons help you determine whether a person is logged into Sametime and available for interaction. In many ways they are like the busy signal or call forwarding on your phone. These icons also display in the Notes client inbox next to the person's name, as well as in other Lotus applications like Quickr and iNotes.

Status icon display	Icon image	What the icon means
"I am available"		The "green light" indicates the person is online and available for chat.
"I am away"		The "yellow light" indicates the person is online but is not available for chat. If you chat with a person with this status, the chat conversation will display in their chat window.
"I'm in a meeting""		The meeting indicator shows that the person is online but is in a meeting. If the user is in a Sametime meeting, other attendees will see the person as online.

Status icon display	Icon image	What the icon means
"Do not disturb"	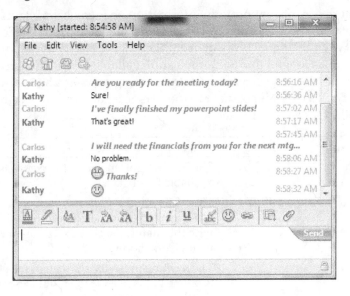	The "red light" indicates that the person is logged into Sametime, but does not want to be contacted. Your privacy settings can also be set so that your status shows "Do not disturb" to some individuals.
No icon displayed		Indicates that the person is not logged into Sametime and thus unavailable to chat.

Starting a chat with a contact

Matt has logged into Sametime. He's added contacts to his Sametime contact list. Now he wants to begin chatting! How do you initiate a chat? First, remember to check a person's Sametime status. If the status icon indicates they're available for a chat session, you're ready to go!

Double-click on the person's name and the basic chat window will appear. Simply start typing in the box at the bottom of the chat window and click on the **Send** button when you're finished. It's good chat etiquette to send a greeting first when initiating a chat just in case the person may be unavailable to chat. Just as you added contacts, you can right-click on the person's name from the **Domino Address Book** or from your inbox to display the option to **Chat**. As a conversation starts, your chat window may begin looking like this:

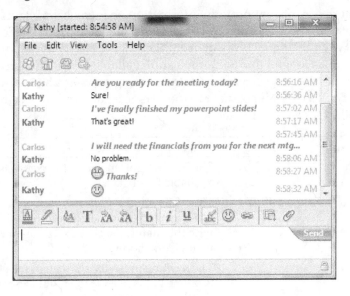

Summary

You now know how to recognize when you have the embedded Sametime client installed and available. You can log into Sametime, configure Sametime single sign-on, determine a person's Sametime status, access your **Preferences** menu, change Sametime to work in your own style, and add contacts to your Sametime contacts list. Finally, you can start a basic chat in Sametime and communicate with anyone who is logged into Sametime.

3

Getting Connected: Configuring and Using Sametime Connect

Sametime Connect is the stand-alone Sametime client that you can use to connect with Sametime networks without using Lotus Notes for e-mail. The Sametime Connect client is as functional as the embedded client and is available for Windows, Mac, and Linux systems.

In this chapter, you'll learn how to:

- Install the Sametime Connect client on a Windows, Mac, or Linux desktop
- Set up the connection to the Sametime server
- Log into and out of the Sametime Connect client
- Set up user preferences
- Install Sametime Connect add-ons for additional Sametime functionality
- Upgrade your Sametime Connect client

Installing Sametime Connect on Windows

Installing Sametime Connect on a Windows desktop is similar to installing any other Windows software. In order to run Sametime your workstation will need to meet the minimum hardware and operating system requirements. If you're unsure about your hardware or operating system, be sure to check with your system administrator.

Hardware requirements	Operating System requirements
CPU – 1GHz (or higher)	Microsoft Windows XP Professional, Service Pack (SP) 2 (or a later SP)
RAM – 512 MB random access memory minimum; 1 GB or higher strongly recommended for Video chat.	Microsoft Windows XP Professional 64-bit Note: only for Web Conferencing; current support for 64-bit Windows XP clients is limited to 32-bit applications (browser and JRE), running in a 64-bit OS environment
256 color video display minimum; 16-bit color or higher recommended.	Microsoft Windows 2000 Pro, SP4 (or a later SP) Microsoft Windows Vista

You'll need a copy of the installation software, which is typically a file that ends in .EXE. Locate the file via Windows Explorer, and begin the installation by double-clicking on the `setup.exe` file. After a language option screen, you will see the Sametime Connect client installation welcome screen to start your install process.

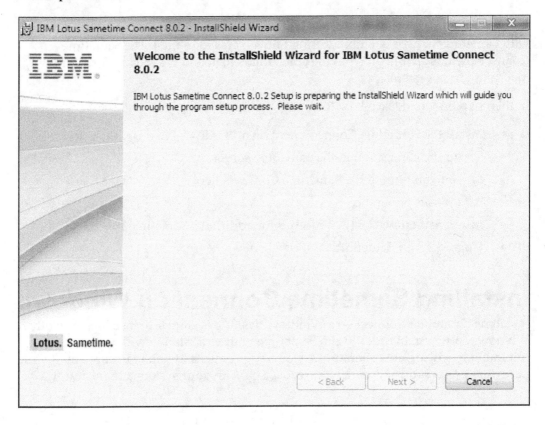

Click on **Next** to proceed. After a License screen (in which you select the **I Accept** option and click on **Next**), you will have the choice of where your install of Sametime Connect should be placed:

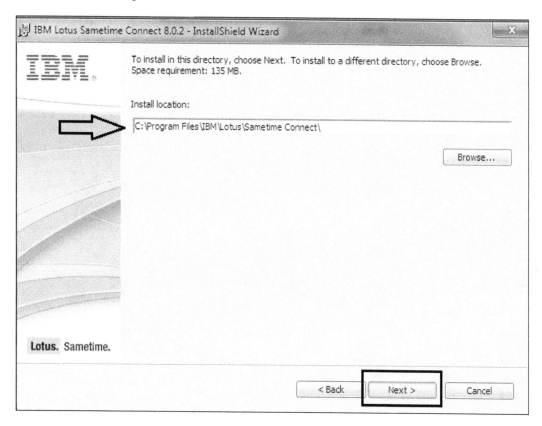

You will see one final screen to confirm you are ready to start your install:

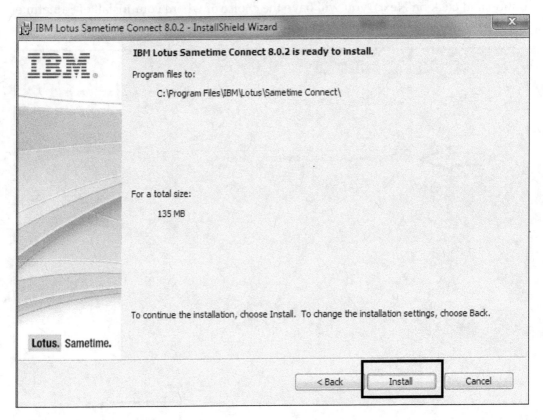

If everything seems correct, click on the **Install** button to start the process. The Windows installer will run for a few minutes, and will successfully install the software in the location you have specified. Once it has installed, you will see a message telling you the installation was successful, and also offering to launch the Sametime Connect software for you:

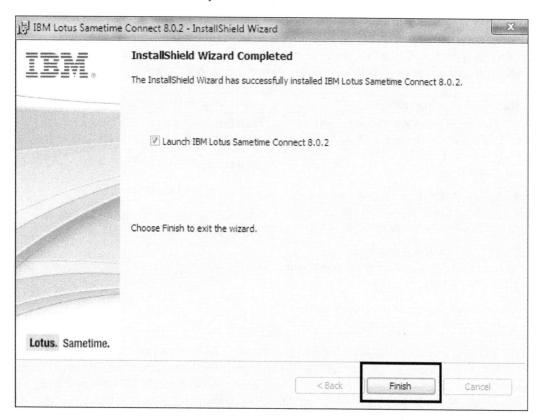

Assuming you leave the **Launch** option selected, Sametime Connect will start and take you to the Sametime sign on screen.

Installing Sametime Connect on a Macintosh

Mac users can also install Sametime Connect. That's one really nice feature of the Sametime Connect client—you have options as to which operating system you can use. So if you use Windows at work, but have a Mac at home, you can still stay connected to your Sametime buddies. And as with the Windows environment, your Macintosh will need to meet the minimum hardware and operating system requirements in order to run Sametime. We've listed them here.

Hardware requirements	Operating System requirements
CPU—Minimum of any PowerPC or Intel CPU supporting Macintosh OSX 10.4.6 (Tiger) with JVM 1.5; 1 GHz CPU, or higher recommended.	Macintosh OS 10.4.x with JVM 1.5, including patches for PowerPC and Intel.
	Macintosh OS 10.5
RAM—512 MB random access memory minimum; 1 GB or higher strongly recommended for Video chat.	**Notes on Macintosh clients:**
	Audio/Video is not currently supported on Macintosh meeting room clients.
Disk space—1GB free disk space recommended to allow space for meetings; 500 MB minimum.	
256 color video display minimum; 16-bit color or higher recommended.	

The following versions of the Macintosh operating system can run the Sametime Connect client: OSX 10.4.x and OSX 10.5. To install the Mac Sametime Connect client, you will need the `sametime-connect.pkg` file or the file specific to the version of Sametime supported in your environment. You begin by clicking on the `.pkg` file which will launch the Sametime installer.

Click on **Continue** to proceed through the license and language agreements until you reach the screen to choose the install directory. You can choose to install Sametime in a directory other than the default, but the default is usually a good choice.

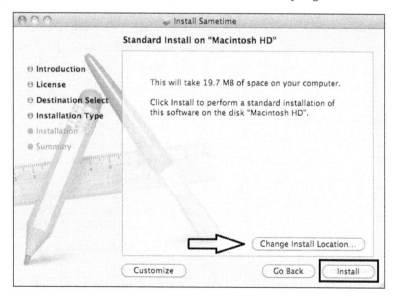

Once you've decided on the install location, click on **Install** to proceed. If your install is successful, you'll see the following screen. You'll also see a Sametime icon in your applications folder on the Mac.

Installing Sametime Connect on Linux

Installing Sametime Connect on a Linux desktop is just as easy as installing Sametime Connect on any other desktop. We've included the minimum hardware and operating system requirements as follows:

Hardware requirements	Operating System requirements
CPU—1GHz (or higher)	SUSE Linux Enterprise Desktop (SLED) 10
RAM—512 MB random access memory minimum; 1 GB or higher recommended.	Novell Linux Desktop (NLD) 9
256 color video display minimum; 16-bit color or higher recommended.	RedHat Enterprise Linux (RHEL) 4.0, 5.0, 5.1, or 5.2
	Notes on Linux clients:
	Audio within Sametime Connect client is supported only on RHEL v5.1 or v5.2
	Clients using RHEL 5.x must enable the following RPM before installing Lotus Sametime Connect to ensure compatibility: compat-libstdc++-33-3.2.3-61.i386.rpm
	Audio/Video is not currently supported on Linux Meeting room clients.
	Video within Sametime Connect is not supported on Linux clients

You'll need a copy of the installation software, typically a file that ends with an .RPM suffix. Here is an example of what it looks like on a SuSE Linux desktop:

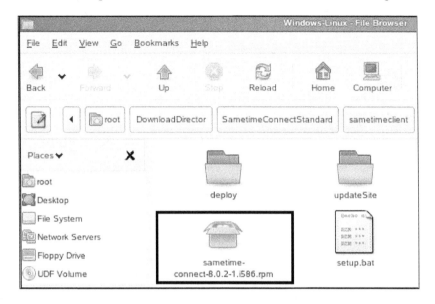

Double-click on the `sametime-connect-8.0.2-1.i586.rpm` file to start the installation. A dialog box appears listing the name of the software that will be installed, along with a checkmark next to it to specify that it's the correct item. When you're ready, click on the **Install** button to start the process:

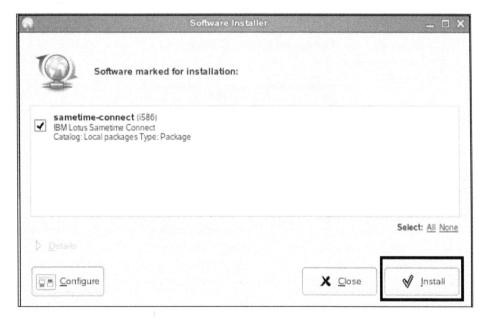

The installer will run for a few minutes and come back with a message saying the installation was successful.

Once that is done, all that's left to do is to launch Sametime Connect from your desktop application menu:

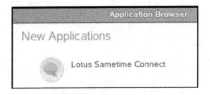

When Sametime launches for the very first time, you'll see the Sametime splash screen and you'll be required to respond to the licensing agreement dialog box. Type **1** to accept the agreement or press *Enter* to read the license agreement. Once you have agreed to the licensing agreement, the sign-on screen for the Sametime Connect client will be displayed. At that point, you will have the sign-on screen for the Connect client, and it will work just like any other version of Sametime Connect.

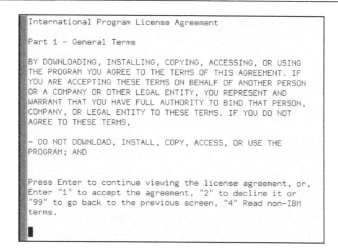

```
International Program License Agreement

Part 1 - General Terms

BY DOWNLOADING, INSTALLING, COPYING, ACCESSING, OR USING
THE PROGRAM YOU AGREE TO THE TERMS OF THIS AGREEMENT. IF
YOU ARE ACCEPTING THESE TERMS ON BEHALF OF ANOTHER PERSON
OR A COMPANY OR OTHER LEGAL ENTITY, YOU REPRESENT AND
WARRANT THAT YOU HAVE FULL AUTHORITY TO BIND THAT PERSON,
COMPANY, OR LEGAL ENTITY TO THESE TERMS. IF YOU DO NOT
AGREE TO THESE TERMS,

- DO NOT DOWNLOAD, INSTALL, COPY, ACCESS, OR USE THE
PROGRAM; AND


Press Enter to continue viewing the license agreement, or,
Enter "1" to accept the agreement, "2" to decline it or
"99" to go back to the previous screen, "4" Read non-IBM
terms.
```

Setting up the connection to the Sametime server

Now that you have Sametime installed, you'll need to log into it. You will have the Sametime icon on your desktop or in your start menu, depending on the operating system you are using. Launching Sametime will open up the logon dialog box:

A few essential pieces of information are needed to complete this dialog box, which they should be provided to you by your technical department, namely **Host server**, **User name**, and **Password**. The Host server field is the Sametime server name. As your contacts connect to this server, you can see when they are available for chatting by the status icons that appear by their names. Your username is normally the same name or user id you use to sign on to your Lotus Notes client, but you may have a separate user id for Sametime depending on the type of authentication Sametime is using. Your password is most likely the same as your Notes client id password, but your technical department should provide you with this information.

If you want to automatically logon when you start up Sametime, select the **Remember Password** and **Automatically log in** checkboxes. This combination ensures that you will automatically sign into Sametime whenever you start up the application. And while this says "automatically", it's important to remember to keep your password up-to-date. The password in the dialog box will require an update for your login to Sametime to be successful.

Once you have completed the dialog box, click on **Log In**, and if your login information is correct, your Sametime client will show you connected to the server:

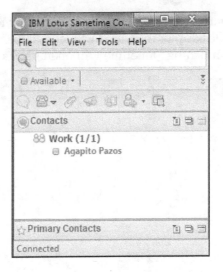

Setting up user preferences

Sametime offers many features that allow you to create a collaborative chat environment that is easy-to-use and manage. Because instant messaging can be used in so many different ways, Sametime includes options for you to modify individual user settings so that Sametime works best for you.

Here are some scenarios:

- Susan works with different Sametime communities, including her work community and remote communities. She can set her preferences for how those connections are displayed in the Sametime toolbar.

- Chen is currently working on a project and only wants his status to display to certain individuals who are working on the project with him. Privacy settings allow him to choose who can see when he's online.

- Because he has additional emoticons or smilies that he likes to include in his chats, Sean can add them via the **Emoticons** settings in his Sametime preferences.

- Mariska travels frequently for her job. When she's in a different time zone or region, she'd like to be able to indicate that on her Sametime status. She can update her **Geographic Location** setting, so her contacts can see from her chat status that her location has changed.

You can customize Sametime to meet these requirements and more! To display the **Preference** menu, select **File | Preferences** (**File | Preferences** for Linux, **Sametime | Preferences** for Mac) from the menu options at the top of the Sametime Connect client. This will bring up the following Sametime Preferences dialog box. Many of these options don't require any changes, but you can make selections to customize Sametime to work the way you want at any time. The **Preferences** window is shown in the following screenshot:

The options are as follows:

- **Accessibility** - contains settings to make Sametime easier to use with screen readers for visually impaired users.

- **Accounts** - stores the login information for any Sametime add-on components that require that additional information.

- **Auto-Status Changes** - controls the conditions under which Sametime will automatically change your status (**Available**, **Away**, **In A Meeting**, and **Do Not Disturb**) or log you off during periods of inactivity.

- **Chat History** - controls how Sametime will save your chat transcripts for you.

- **Chat Window** - controls how the Sametime chat window will appear, as well as font settings, time stamps, and how certain keystrokes are interpreted.

- **Contact List** - controls how Sametime will notify you during certain contact list activities, as well as how your contact list will be maintained and stored on the Sametime server.

- **Emoticon Palettes** - lists the active emoticons, or small graphic images to help convey emotions, in your Sametime client. You can also add or remove additional emoticon palettes here.

- **External Applications** - stores the external mail application you use so that Sametime can communicate with it.

- **File Transfers** - controls where files transferred during a Sametime chat will be stored.

- **Geographic Location** - maintains geographical information about where you are as well as contact information about you. This information is displayed at the top of your Sametime profile and chats.

- **Language** - controls the language that Sametime will use for the menus and screens.

- **Notification** - controls the sounds that Sametime will make when certain events occur.

- **Privacy** - controls who can see you when you're logged onto Sametime, as well as who can contact you if you're in **Do Not Disturb** mode.

- **Server Communities** - contains all the technical information about how your Sametime client will connect to one or more Sametime servers.

- **Spell Checking** - controls how spellchecking occurs in your Sametime client, and what dictionary language should be used for the spellchecking.

- **Status Messages** - specifies the basic status messages that are displayed when you are in **Available, Away, In A Meeting**, and **Do Not Disturb** mode. It also controls if you are given the option to edit the status message each time your status changes.

- **Telephony, Audio and Video** - controls the microphone, speaker, and video camera settings for your Sametime client if you have those available to use.

- **Web Conference Tools** - indicates what tools (microphone, speaker, and camera) you have available for web conferences.

Don't be overwhelmed by all the choices you have for configuring Sametime. As you become more of a Sametime expert, you'll know exactly what options you want or need to change to customize and streamline Sametime into your very own personalized instant messaging client.

Installing Sametime Connect add-ons

Another valuable feature of Sametime Connect is add-ons, also known as plug-ins. Plug-ins are features you can install from IBM or other vendors that extend and enhance your Sametime client. For instance:

- Jessie uses the Calculator application on his desktop frequently, but it would be very convenient if there was a calculator in his Sametime Connect client so that he didn't have to keep two different applications running.

In this situation, Jessie is in luck as a company named Epilio has a calculator plug-in for Sametime. In the following steps, we are going to install that plug-in. These same steps can be followed to install any plug-in that works with Sametime.

In your Sametime Connect client, start the plug-in installation feature from the menu option **Tools | Plug-ins | Install Plug-ins**. A dialog box will appear, allowing you to select the option to **Search For New Features To Install** and click on **Next**.

From the Epilio website, we can see that the plug-ins are found at an update site located at `http://www.epilio.com/stupdate.nsf/site.xml`. So we click on the **Add Remote Location** button, give the update site a name such as Epilio Plug-ins (this can actually be any name you want it to be), and then add the URL of the update site. Click on the **OK** button.

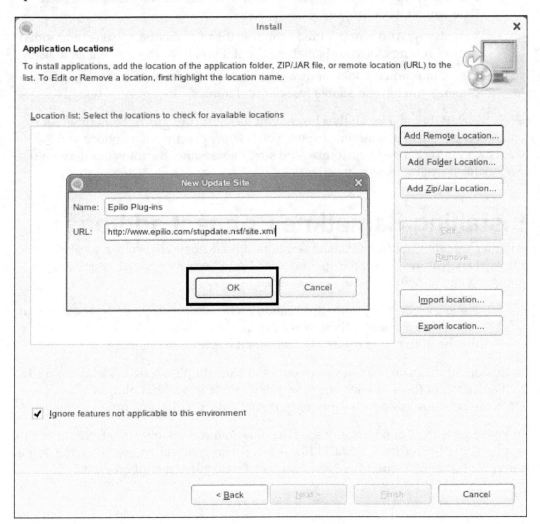

The resulting screen will show the name of the update site you provided, and you click on **Finish**.

Sametime accesses the update site and returns a list of all the Sametime plug-ins that you can select. In this case, we select the **Epilio Calculator** and click on **Next**.

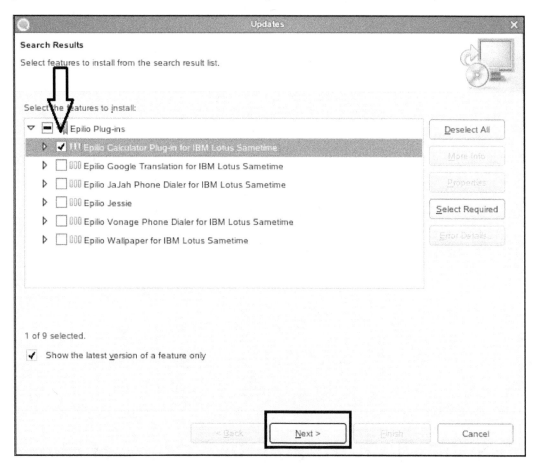

Sametime will confirm that you selected the items you wanted, and you click on **Finish**. You will need to close and restart the Sametime Connect client when the installation is finished. After you log back into Sametime, you will now have a new feature in your Sametime Connect client — the Epilio Calculator!

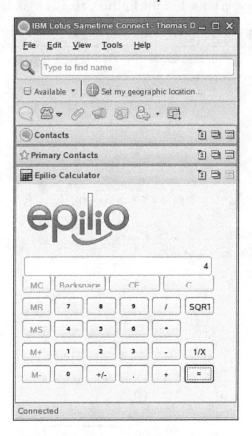

Upgrading Your Sametime Connect client

Much like all other software you use, IBM releases periodic upgrades to the Sametime software. But fortunately, upgrading your Sametime client is extremely easy, and you won't lose any of your contacts or information.

How you upgrade your software will depend on how your technical administration staff chooses to distribute the upgrade. They could provide you with the installation file in which you would install the new version of Sametime Connect just like you installed it originally. The installation software will detect where the existing version of the Sametime software is installed, and will install the update in the same place, overlaying the old version with the new version.

The other method of upgrading your Sametime client involves having the administrators "push" the upgrade to you the next time you sign in. When the administrators use this method, they change a setting on the Sametime server that informs your Sametime client that updates are available. Those updates get sent over the network to you, and the installation occurs automatically. You don't have to click on any files or figure out how to install it.

The important thing to remember is that with either method, you won't lose anything that you already have installed. You'll open your Sametime Connect client like you always do, and you can continue to work just like you always have.

Summary

In this chapter, you learned how to install the Sametime Connect client using Windows, Linux, and Mac operating systems. You learned how to connect to the Sametime server and how to set user preferences. You also learned how to install plug-ins within your Sametime Connect client as well as how to upgrade the Sametime client.

4

Managing Your Connections: Making the most of your Sametime Contacts

With your Sametime client up and running, you'd like to start chatting with your colleagues. To do so, you need to add their names to your contact list. Once someone is in your contact list, you can start communicating and collaborating with them in a number of different ways.

In this chapter, you'll learn how to:

- Add and remove people from your contact list
- Understand the different types of directory entries you might encounter
- Create nicknames for the people on your contact list
- Categorize your contacts into different groups
- Sort your contacts and groups
- Manage groups and contacts between different types of Sametime clients
- Use "type-ahead" on your contact list
- Display a contact's business card
- Manage your online presence when you're on Sametime
- Create group chats between three or more contacts

Managing your contacts

Let's start managing your contact list by adding the names of those colleagues or friends you would like to chat with on a regular basis. By adding them to your contact list, you can easily see their availability status whether they are online and available to chat, offline, or online but away from their desk.

In our examples, we're going to assume that you're a new user just beginning to use Sametime and starting to set up your contact list. We're going to walk you through the different processes and tricks that you can use to get you up and running to chat with other people.

Some usage scenarios include the following:

- George is a new Sametime user and has no contacts in his contact list but he wants to start contacting users quickly.

- Susan has many users but she wants to sort them alphabetically and arrange them into groups. She also wants to have some flexibility for displaying how the users appear.

- Rob travels for his job and works from multiple workstations. He wants to be sure that if he makes changes on one workstation, his contact list will be up-to-date on the other workstation.

- Chia has many groups in his contact list. He wants to chat with multiple users at one time in a group window as he's working on a group project requiring input from all team members.

Contact list and "type ahead"

Have you ever wanted to quickly find a name in your contact list? Or perhaps start a chat quickly without looking up at a person's name? You can use one of Sametime's advanced features called "type ahead." This process anticipates the name you are looking for by searching in your contact list for the closest matches while you are typing. This is useful if you have a lengthy contact list and want to simply type the first few letters of a person's name when you want to begin chatting with them. All you need to do is start typing the name in the search area of the Sametime client. The matches to the names will begin to appear. The more letters you type, the narrower the search will become.

Adding contacts

While you can take advantage of the "type ahead" feature, you can also create your own personal lists. These may be organized by teams, departments, or locations. Their organization is up to you. To add someone to your list, click on the drop-down arrow on the right-side of the icon bar, and then click on **New | New Sametime Contact**:

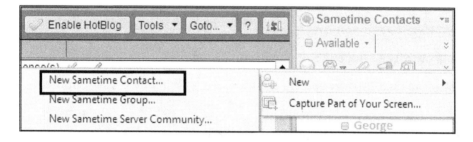

The **Add Sametime Contact** dialog box will display. In this dialog box, type in the name of the person you want to add. You can type in their name or any part of their name and click on the **Lookup** button. In this case, you typed in the full name of **Sandra Woolfolk** and received her name back as the only match in the returned list of names. To add her to your list of Sametime contacts, click on her name to select it, and then click on the **Add** button at the bottom of the dialog box:

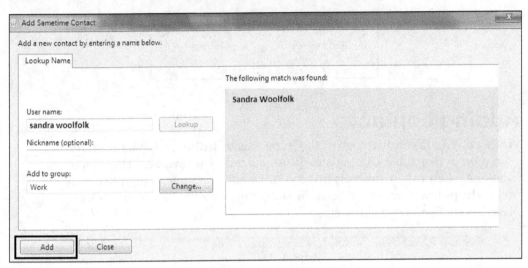

Sandra is now listed in your Sametime contact list.

If you want to do a broader search, you can also type in any part of Sandra's name, such as just her last name. Sametime searches the directory for all the matches on the partial name, and returns them for your selection. In this example, the search for Sandra's last name returned more than one name.

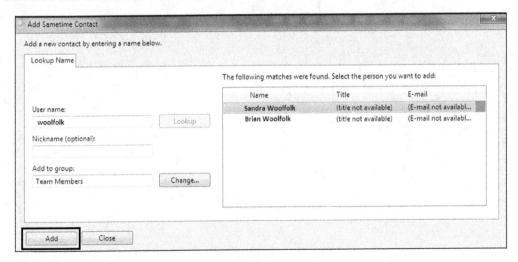

The selection process to add Sandra to your contact list is the same as before. Select her name by clicking on it, and then click on the **Add** button. Remember to select the appropriate group in which to add the person. You can always change your mind and reorganize your contact list, but it's better to get this right on the first try.

As you've learned thus far with Sametime, there are multiple ways to go about completing a task. Selecting names is no exception. Another way to add Sandra to your contact list is by using the search bar. In the blank line, you begin by typing her name and the dialog box will list matches as you begin to type. Once you see a match for Sandra's full name, you can right-click on her name and select the **Add To Sametime Contact List** option:

You can also right-click on a group name in your contact list and this will return a pop-up menu with the **Add Contact** option available.

Adding contacts from your inbox

With Lotus Notes, if you are using the Sametime Embedded client, you can also add contacts from your inbox. When you receive a new message, you can add the person to your contact list by right-clicking on the e-mail, selecting the person's name, and then selecting the option to **Add to Sametime Contact List**.

In the Notes client, you can also drag-and-drop a name from your inbox into the Sametime contact list. To do this, select an e-mail ID and drag-and-drop onto a group name. Once you do that the **Add Sametime Contact** dialog box will display. This dialog is slightly different than the previous **Add Sametime Contact** dialog in that it may show additional possible matches to the name. You'll notice that you can modify a Nickname, as well as specify the group name in which to add the user.

In this screen you see that you can also change the Sametime server community. A Sametime "server community" is a group of Sametime users who can communicate with each other. The Sametime client can connect to multiple Sametime communities, making it simpler for you to communicate with your colleagues who may be in different companies or locations from one central place—your Sametime client! Your Sametime administrator may have configured your Sametime client to connect to several communities at once. But if you are only connected to one Sametime server community—your default community—you won't see this as an option.

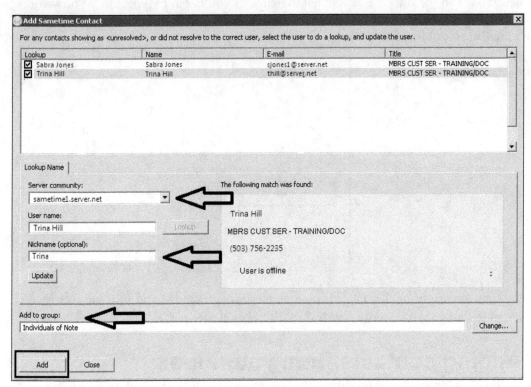

Removing contacts

Suppose you've added a name to your Sametime contact list that you no longer need to chat with on a regular basis. You can remove that contact as easily as you added the person. You simply right-click on the name of the person you want to remove. A pop-up menu with an option to remove the name with the **Remove from Sametime Contact List** option will display:

When you select that option, the person is removed from your contact list. Be sure you want to remove the person as there is no undo function. Another option for "uncluttering" your contact list might be to move this person to a different group.

Importing and exporting contacts

In the Sametime Connect client, you have the option of importing or exporting an existing contact list. Your Sametime administrator may have provided you with an import file that includes contacts and several public groups, or you may have exported your contact list prior to uninstalling Sametime. To begin either process, select the **File | Import Contact List or File | Export Contact List** option. You can import your contact list from either your Sametime community or a local .dat file. Your Sametime export options include exporting as a multiple community file (all community contacts are included in one file) as an .xml file, or individual community files (each Sametime community's contacts are separated) in a .dat file.

Displaying online contacts

You may find it easier to sort through your contacts if you are only displaying colleagues who are available to chat or who are logged into Sametime. You can change your Sametime contacts list to only show people who are online by right-clicking on any of the Group names in your contact list. A pop-up menu appears that has an option to **Show Online Only**:

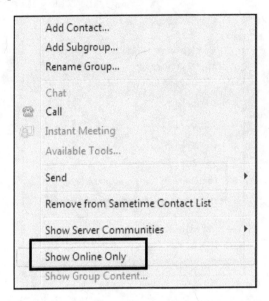

When you select that option, a checkmark appears next to the option, indicating your contact list will only display those individuals who are online in Sametime. If you repeat the process, the checkmark will disappear, and everyone on your list will once again appear, regardless of whether they are signed on or not. This option is also available from the Notes client, **View | Sametime | Online Contacts Only**.

Setting preferences for contacts

The Sametime Preferences screen has a number of settings that allow you to control how your contact list displays information or alerts you to various changes. You can control the font settings of the contact list, whether offline contacts show up on your list, how your contact list synchronizes if the local version is different than the server version, and other settings. Most of the settings are self-explanatory, and you can experiment with them without any risk of damage as you can always use the **Restore Default** button to reset the options to the way they were when you first installed Sametime.

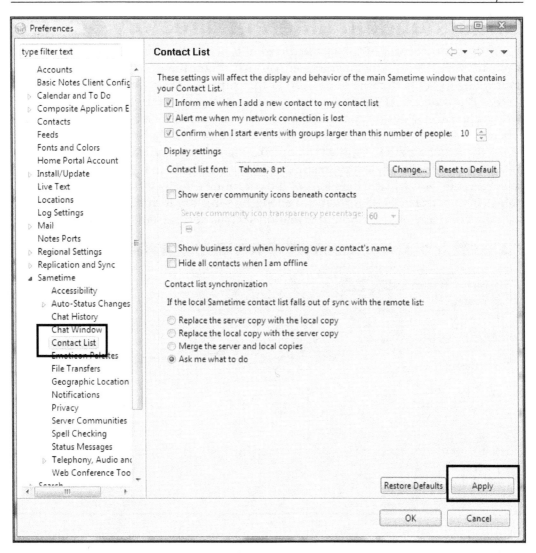

Understanding different directory types

Your Sametime server can connect to different types of directories for contact name lookups. Depending on your company's configuration, Sametime might be connecting to Lotus Domino or to a server that supports **Lightweight Directory Access Protocol (LDAP)**. If you're not sure about your directory type you can ask your technical staff for further information. If a directory is available for searching, when you choose to search for a person's name, you will see a **Browse for Name** tab in the **Add Sametime Contact** dialog box. The **Browse for Name** tab will not be available if your Sametime administrator has not enabled that feature. When you select this tab, you will see the name of the corporate directory as well as the users' names in both a shortened format and a lengthy directory format, which usually includes company organization information such as department or company name.

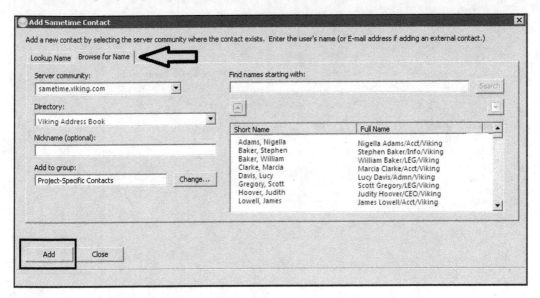

Contact nicknames

When you add names to your contact list, they appear using the name of the person as it is stored in the address book used by Sametime. If you don't want all the corporate or department related information included with someone's name, you can change how the names appear in your contact list. Nicknames are also useful for the "type ahead" feature as once a nickname has been created, you simply have to begin typing the nickname and Sametime will find your contact for you. For the Sametime Embedded client, select **View | Sametime | Short Names** and for the Sametime Connect client, select **View | Short Names**. This allows you to only have the shorter names displayed in your contact list, without the corporate directory information.

It might be easier for you to recognize a contact if the displayed name for your contact uses the same name you use for the person instead of their full formal name. For instance, you may know your coworker Gabriella by the name Gab. You would like to see that name appear in the contact list instead. Fortunately, Sametime lets you assign an alternative name, or a "nickname", to your contact. When you are adding Gabriella to your contact list, you can give her the nickname of Gab at that point:

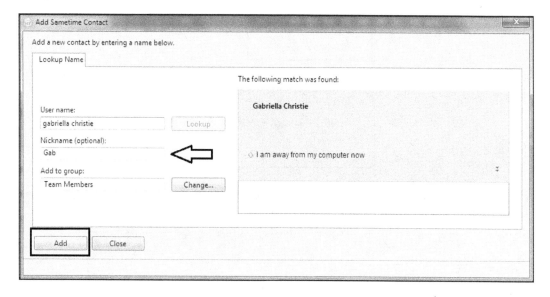

Once you click on **Add**, you will now see Gabriella show up in your contact list as Gab:

You can also change Gab's name once it is on your contact list. If you right-click on her name, you can choose the option from the pop-up menu to **Edit Nickname**:

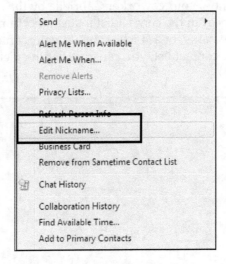

This action returns a dialog box that lets you enter the new name by which you want this contact to be identified on your contact list:

Enter Gab's last name and click on **OK**. You now see her new nickname on your contact list:

Managing contacts with contact groups

If you have a large number of contacts in your contact list, it might be time consuming to find the name of the person with whom you want to chat. In this situation, Sametime can help you categorize those names by putting them into Contact Groups. For instance, you may want to have some contacts grouped together as Team Members, while others are grouped together as part of a project team to which you belong.

If you were to go back to the original **Add Contact** dialog box, it showed the field labeled **Add To Group**. This field allows you to add your new contact to a group on your contact list. This can either be a new group or an existing group:

If you didn't remember to add a person to a group when you added a contact in the first place, you don't have to delete your contact and start over. You can create the new groups in your contact list and start moving people into those groups.

To create a new group, you can right-click on a group name in the Sametime contact list which returns a pop-up menu with the option to **Add Subgroup**. The dialog box then allows you to add a new personal group, search for an existing public group, and decide if the new group should be a subgroup under an existing group:

Let's say you are going to create a new group called **Team Members** where you can add the people who are on your work team. You've decided that it should be a top level group instead of one listed under another group, like the default Work group.

When you click on **OK**, you will see the new group in your Contact list:

You also have the option to search for a public group. A public group could be a distribution list that's part of your corporate Sametime directory. By adding a public group to your contact list, everyone in that group will appear under that group name in your contact list. This is ideal if the group changes often, or includes many members so that you won't have to maintain the list yourself. Your contact list will stay up-to-date with the current members of the group. Membership of the public group is maintained by your Sametime administrator or the managers of your corporate directory. You cannot change the membership of the public group you added, nor can you add new members to that group. The people who appear in your contact list under public groups will stay synchronized in your contact lists as members are added to and removed from the corporate directory group. While you can't modify a public group, they are still useful, especially in large organizations where you are trying to follow the online status of many individuals whom you may not know very well.

Now that you've added the new group, how can you get new people into that group, or how do you move people out of one group and into another? It's very easy! You can drag names between your personal groups. As we said earlier, you cannot add new names to Public groups, but you can drag names from Public groups to your own groups if you so choose. You click the name of the contact that needs to be moved, and then drag the name under the new group. You now see the name in the new location.

You can also add the person to your contact list again, so that they appear under multiple groups. This is helpful if you generally expand and collapse your groups based on what project you are currently working on, and your contacts are part of that particular project.

Sorting the group or contact list

As you add more contacts and groups to your contact list, you may want to sort the list. By default, the groups and contacts are sorted in the order in which they are added. You can sort them from the Notes client by selecting **View | Sametime | Contacts Alphabetically** or **View | Sametime Groups Alphabetically**.

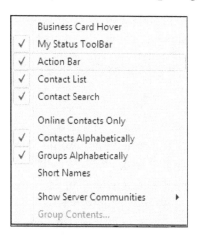

The Sametime Connect client also has an option for sorting contacts and groups. Select **View | Groups Alphabetically** or **View | Contacts Alphabetically** to sort your groups and contacts.

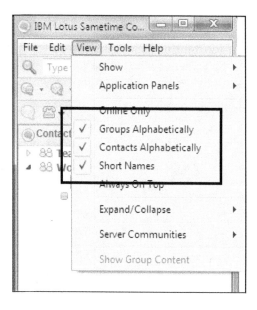

Managing groups and contacts between different Sametime clients

If you work from multiple workstations and locations, you don't have to worry about merging your Sametime contact lists between locations. You definitely don't want to lose your contact list especially since you've customized it. That's why your contact list is stored on the Sametime server. And because the contacts and groups are stored on the Sametime server, you might see the Contact List Conflict Message dialog box when you log into Sametime from another workstation. This dialog is displayed when the contact list on one of your clients doesn't match what is stored on the server.

You'll be prompted to:

- Replace the version of the contact list on the Sametime server with the current version you're working with on your local computer
- Replace the version of the contact list on your local computer with the most current version stored on the Sametime server
- Or merge the server and local versions into one contact list

You're most likely to see this message after you've made lots of changes to your contacts such as deleting, renaming, or organizing them into groups. When you login to another workstation which might not have your most recent contact changes, the conflict message dialog will display. Respond carefully as you can't undo this change once you make your selection.

You do have the option of setting this as a preference, so that it is always set to do one action consistently. If you always want to be prompted, select this option in the **Contact List** preferences in your Sametime preferences.

Contact list synchronization

If the local Sametime contact list falls out of sync with the remote list:

- Replace the server copy with the local copy
- Replace the local copy with the server copy
- Merge the server and local copies
- Ask me what to do

Contact lists and business card information

Your Sametime administrator may have customized your chat environment to include "business card" information about you in your chat profile. You have the ability to display this information for your contacts or hide it as it does take up space in the chat window. This information can be useful as it may contain a phone number, title, or department name. The Sametime business card may also include a photo of the individual. The photo can be useful in so many ways—you may never have met your Sametime contact in person, or there may be multiple matches on the name, but you only know the person by sight. Including a photo also helps to "personalize" the chat so you don't feel like you're only chatting to an icon or a name.

To begin seeing the business card information in your chat window, you need to make some changes to your Sametime settings. For the Embedded Client, go to **File | Preferences | Sametime | Chat Window** and select **Display chat partner's business card in the chat window**.

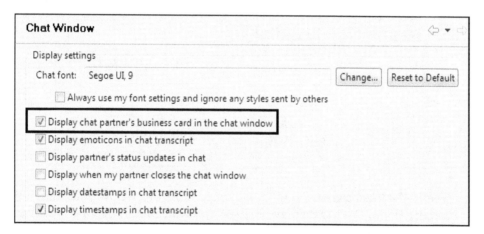

If you'd like to see the business card info when you move your mouse or "hover" over your contact's name, this setting needs to be selected as well. From the Embedded Client go to **File | Preferences | Sametime | Contact List** and select **Show business card when hovering over a contact's name**.

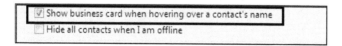

You can also make these settings changes in the Sametime Connect client. Open a chat window and select **View | Show | Business Card** to enable the business card option. The check mark by the option indicates that it is enabled.

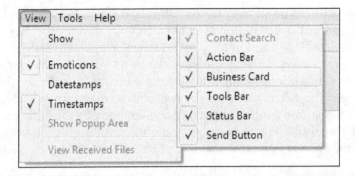

You can also enable the ability to hover over business card information in the Sametime Connect client. Select **View | Show | Hover Business Cards** to enable this function.

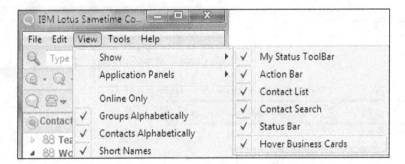

So what might the business card info look like? It depends on how your Sametime server has been configured to display business card information. Hover business card information is displayed when you move your mouse over a contact's name and might look something like this:

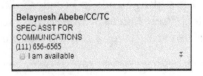

Wouldn't this be helpful if you're quickly trying to find a phone number for your contact or his/her title? Yes! Business card information can also display in a chat window. This might include a person's picture.

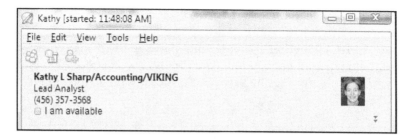

Managing your online presence

Even though you are logged into Sametime, there are times when you want your contacts and others in your organization to know you are available and other times when you may not want to be disturbed. Or, you may want to let people know you are away from your desk for a period of time. Sametime lets you do this, as well as letting you specify who can see that you're online. So let's see how you can manage your status or "online presence".

Sametime status settings

When you sign on to Sametime, your status will be set to **Available**. That's the green square you see next to your name. You can change your status by clicking on the **Available** status button at the top of your Sametime client:

In addition to showing that you're in the **I Am Available** status, you also have the option to choose from **I Am Away**, **In A Meeting**, and **Do Not Disturb**. To select any of those options, you simply click on that status, and the icon and status message changes to reflect the updated status.

If you select **I Am Away**, your status changes to **Away** with a yellow diamond icon. Switching to **In A Meeting** changes your status to the same wording and adds a little calendar icon next to your name. And finally, if you choose **Do Not Disturb**, your status wording changes to the same thing, along with a stop sign icon next to your name.

Status icon display	Icon image	What the icon means
"I am available"		The "green light" indicates the person is online and available for chat.
"I am away"		The "yellow light" indicates the person is online but is not available for chat. If you chat with a person with this status, the chat conversation will display in their chat window.
"I'm in a meeting"		The meeting indicator shows that the person is online but is in a meeting. If the user is in a Sametime meeting, other attendees will see the person as online.
"Do not disturb"		The "red light" indicates that the person is logged into Sametime, but does not want to be contacted. Your privacy settings can also be set so that your status shows "Do not disturb" to some individuals.
No icon displayed		Indicates that the person is not logged into Sametime and thus unavailable to chat.

Why is awareness or online presence so important? It lets your colleagues know when you are available for a conversation. Think of it as your way of setting your Sametime answering machine or "busy signal". When you know you can't chat because you are on a phone call or working on a project, it's wise to change your status, not only for your peace of mind, but for others who might be looking for you.

In our example, when you change your status to **Away** or **In A Meeting**, anyone trying to contact you will get a warning message before the chat box becomes available:

While the person contacting you can still send a chat message, they have been warned that you might not be available to answer right away.

If you change your status to **Do Not Disturb**, Sametime goes one step further and prevents chat messages from being sent to you at all:

The person initiating the chat has the opportunity to send you an e-mail instead, but they won't be able to start a chat. In this way, you can stay focused on what you're trying to do without Sametime becoming a distraction.

If you don't want to be disturbed, why wouldn't you just turn off Sametime altogether? For one reason, being in **Do Not Disturb** status shows others that you are signed on to Sametime, but just can't be reached at the current time. If you were to sign off completely, others may not know if you were in the office or otherwise reachable at a later time. Secondly, there is a way that you can let some people reach you in **Do Not Disturb** mode by updating your Privacy settings, which will be covered shortly.

When someone tries to contact you, they'll be able to see one of four options for your status. But you might like to provide your teammates or colleagues with a bit more information as to what you're currently doing. For instance, you might be away, but would like to let others know that you'll be back at a certain time. You can do this by updating the Status message when you switch status settings.

For example, when you switch to the **Away** status, you'll see a dialog box that allows you to update your status message:

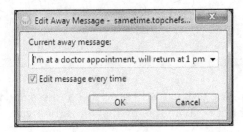

When you click on **OK**, that status message will be shown to others when they try to send a chat message to you. Sametime will also save the last few messages for you to choose from if you click on the drop-down arrow next to the status message. This is useful if there are a number of common status messages that you use, such as "Gone to Lunch" or "Attending daily status meeting".

Changing your status frequently during the course of your day may seem daunting, but it only takes seconds to do, and you'll find that your communication with others will become more effective by doing so.

Sametime also allows you to set some preconfigured defaults for your status messages. You can set these ahead of time, so that they are ready to go based on the type of status you set. From **File | Preferences | Sametime | Status Messages**, you can decide what will be your default status when you first login to Sametime, as well as create messages for your other status changes. You can also change the automatic prompt settings. If you know that when you change your status to **In A Meeting** that you always want your display message to say "I am in a meeting, please contact me through e-mail", you won't be prompted every time you set that status!

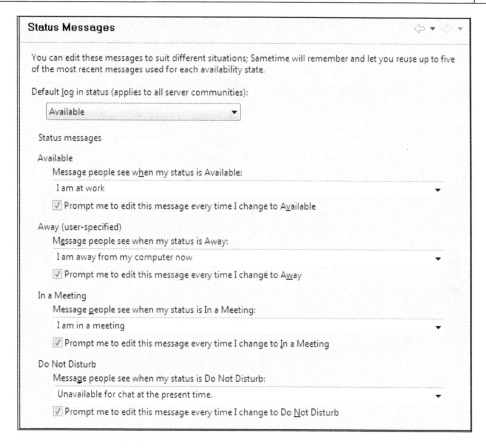

Sametime privacy settings

Let's take status a step further. You are now going to **Do Not Disturb** mode, as you have a report due for your boss in the next hour. But you still need to allow your boss and a coworker to reach you via chat during that time, while locking out everyone else. How can you do that? Simply change your **Privacy** settings in your Sametime preferences.

From the Embedded Sametime client, choose **File | Preferences | Sametime | Privacy** or from the Sametime Connect client, select **File | Preferences | Privacy**, to modify the Privacy options:

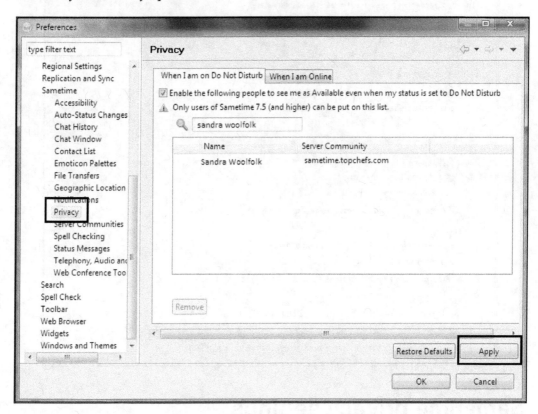

The **Privacy** settings allow you to make exceptions to those who can send you messages while you're in **Do Not Disturb** mode. Enter Sandra's name in the search box and then select it. Once you have selected all the names of the people who should be able to send you messages, click on **Apply**. Those individuals can now initiate a chat with you while everyone else is locked out. So while you are working hard on the report due for your boss, Sandra can still chat with you about project-related topics.

Likewise, you can use the **When I Am Online** tab of the Privacy settings to further control your online presence:

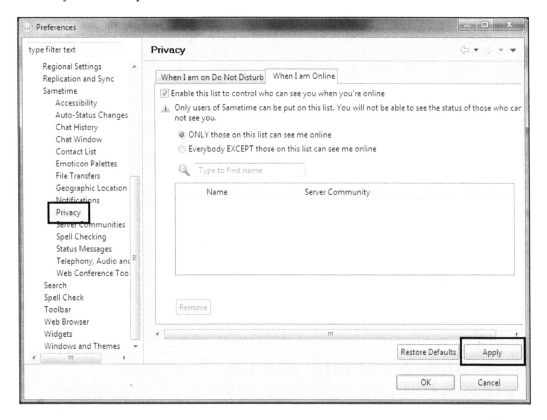

In this tab, you can do one of two things. You can either list only the people who can see you online (regardless of your status), or you can list people who will never see you as being online. That means that everyone would see you when you're online, but these particular people would always see you as being offline.

While this option may seem to be very appealing on those days when you are getting overloaded with chat requests, it's not a good idea to use this on a regular basis. The main purpose of Sametime is to collaborate and communicate with others in your organization. If you start to make it difficult or impossible for people to reach you on a regular basis, any communication that requires your input becomes more difficult and the work that involves you may be delayed because you're unreachable. So you should use this option very carefully and only in rare cases. Be aware that privacy settings are local to the client you are using. If you are working on a project from your home office, you will need to modify the settings as well as those on your workstation at your company's location.

Contact list awareness using alerts

Another useful awareness related option in Sametime is Alerts. You may have someone that you need to contact with an important question but that person is not currently signed on to Sametime. Rather than spending time rechecking your list to see if the contact has signed on yet, you can set an alert to notify you when they arrive. That option is titled **Alert Me When Available** in the pop-up menu when you right-click on the contact's name. When you select this, a little alarm bell icon is put next to the person's name on the contact list. As soon as they sign on, you'll receive a pop-up message alerting you to their presence, and you can contact them immediately at that point.

Sametime automatic status changes

The **Auto-Status Changes** preference allows you to preset Sametime awareness messages in advance. This preference setting allows you to create messages that will be in place when certain events occur. For example, if you are away from your desk and there is no mouse or keyboard activity for a set number of minutes, your awareness status will be automatically changed to **Away** and the hover message will change to **I am away from my computer now**. Once you move the mouse again, the status will revert back to **Active**. These automatic changes are all optional of course, but why not set them and have Sametime manage these actions for you!

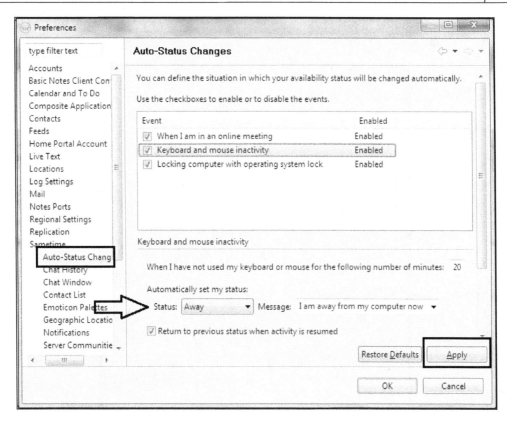

Group chatting

There are times when simply chatting with another person is perfect for the information you need to obtain. But there are other times when you need to be able to chat with more than one person in order to resolve a problem or pass along information. In Sametime this feature is called **Group Chat**.

To start a group chat, you double-click on your own name in your contact list. This starts a normal chat with you as the only participant. You then click on the multiple people icon in the chat icon bar to start inviting more people into the chat:

This launches a dialog box that allows you to specify one or more people who are invited to join you in the chat:

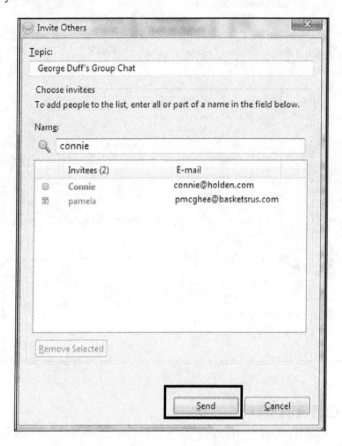

As you type names into the **Name** field, you see them appear in a drop-down list from which you can select the people who should join. Once you have selected all the participants, you click on the **Send** button. Each participant will receive a small pop-up window asking them to join the chat. Once everyone joins, you can begin your group chat and everyone in the group can chat in the same window together:

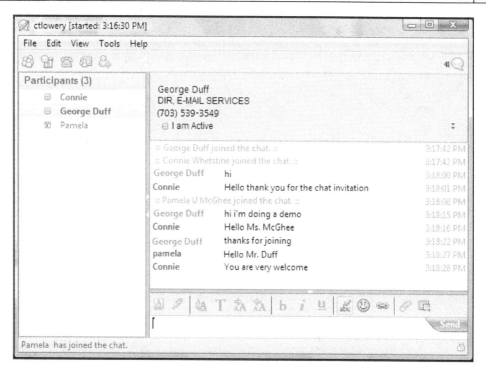

When a member of the chat types a message, a pencil icon is displayed by their name in the participants' window. This notifies everyone in the Group chat as to who is "speaking" or is going to contribute next in the conversation. Group chats are a great way to make sure that everyone is seeing the same information at the same time, and that no information or communication gets lost or misinterpreted. All participants will see status messages about who has joined the chat as well as when individuals have left the group chat.

Summary

In this chapter, you learned how to add and remove contacts from your Sametime contact list. You learned how to manage your online presence and privacy using preferences and alerts within Sametime. You learned how to manage contact groups for putting your contacts into categories. You learned how to customize the display of your contact's name regardless of what directory you might be using and how to display your contact's business card information, as well as how to assign nicknames to your contacts. Finally, you learned how to participate in group chats within Sametime.

5

Power Chatting: Making the most of Sametime Instant Messaging

Now that you have your contact list set up, you're ready to start chatting with your colleagues on Sametime. It's very easy to do basic chatting, but Sametime is capable of so much more. You can use various fonts, images, links, and many other features that are included in Sametime.

In this chapter, you'll learn how to:

- Use rich text and different text styles in your chat messages
- Show date and time stamps to your chat
- Save and view your chat history and transcripts
- Automatically spell-check your chats
- Add graphics and images in your chat
- Add and use emoticons in Sametime
- Add attachments and hyperlinks to your chat messages
- Capture parts of your screen to show it to others in your chat
- Integrate and use Sametime if you're using Microsoft Office, Outlook, or SharePoint
- Use voice and video in during your chats

Spice up your text communication

You've mastered basic chat and your communication and collaboration is working well. But often, plain text doesn't do enough to convey the emotion or context of your message. It's often necessary to go beyond basic text if you're trying to make an important point. Fortunately, Sametime has many different ways to allow you to do just that. For example:

- Kali is heading up a team with a rapidly approaching deadline. She wants to convey to one team member during their online discussions how important it is that the deadline is met.

- Fritz is worried that sometimes his quick typing may be getting him in trouble as he frequently makes typos. He'd like to avoid those especially when he's chatting with his manager.

- Francie is leading a software design project where she needs to display what appears on her workstation to several colleagues all at once. She'd like to be able to do that in real time without having to take multiple screenshots.

- Matt leads a team of auditors who occasionally want to take a chat and turn it into a voice communication without any interruption in their discussion. They are connected to a Sametime Standard server and all of the team members involved have headsets.

Let's get started and familiarize ourselves with the Sametime chat toolbar.

Icon Image	What the icon means
	Changes the foreground text color
	Changes the background text color
	Changes text properties back to default settings.
	Displays text setting dialog box to change text type, size, color, and various other settings.
	Increases the text size by one setting.

Icon Image	What the icon means
	Decreases the text size by one setting.
	Bold text
	Italics text
	Underlined text
	Check spelling
	Insert Emoticon
	Hyperlink
	Capture part of your screen to send to your partner [Available only in the Sametime Standard client set]
	Send a file to your chat partner [Available only in the Sametime Standard client set]

There is one more icon that should be mentioned. You may or may not have noticed the little lock icon in the bottom right-hand corner of your Sametime Embedded or Sametime Connect client. This icon indicates that your chat is encrypted. Why is this important? This means that the chat transmission is secured between you and the Sametime server and between you and the colleagues with whom you are chatting. You don't have to worry about anyone tapping into the chat session and reading your communication.

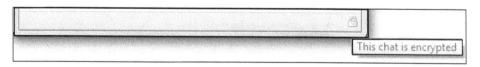

Rich text and text styles

Rather than use the default text in Sametime, you can change the font type and size of your chat using the toolbar in the Sametime chat client. In the following example, Cara wanted to make sure that Mitch knew that her request was very important by underlining, bolding, and italicizing the word "very":

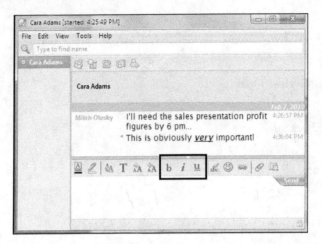

To do this, she highlighted the word "very" and then used the icons located right above her chat text entry area. She clicked the "**b**", "*i*", and "u" icons and then sent the message.

The icons above the chat area allow you to "spice up" your communication in various ways.

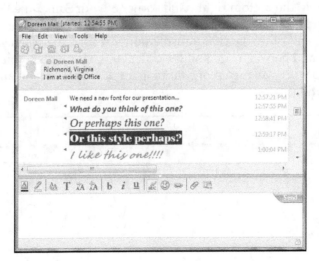

When you use these features by clicking on the icons, it only applies to the specific message you're entering. However, you can make these settings permanent by going to your Sametime preferences and displaying the **Sametime | Chat Window** settings. In the **Display Settings** option group, the first setting allows you to change your font display to whatever you like, and those settings will be used for each successive chat.

Date stamps

When you send a chat to someone or receive a chat message, you might like to know exactly when the chat message was sent. You can do this by turning on the setting that allows Sametime to show the date and time of each chat message. This is especially important if you are maintaining chat transcripts or are tracking responses and are working on deadlines.

You can go to the Sametime preferences screen in **Sametime | Chat Window** to set this feature. The **Display Datestamps in Chat Transcript** and **Display Timestamps in Chat Transcript** options should be selected to get this feature enabled for all your chats.

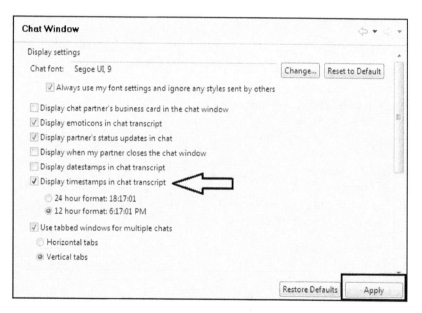

This same preferences screen gives you the option for setting windows for multiple chats. This allows you to control how you want all the chat windows displayed and organized, and is especially important if you are chatting with many colleagues all at one time—each in a different window. You certainly wouldn't want to type the wrong thing in the wrong window!

Chat history

As you continue to have chats over time, you will probably want to be able to refer back to prior chats that you've had with other people. To do that, you'll need to maintain a history of your chat transcripts. In some organizations this may be done automatically at the server level as it may be mandatory for your company due to regulatory constraints. In order to maintain chat transcripts yourself, you need to enable the Chat History feature in Sametime. That feature allows you to view same-day chats with a particular individual, as well as being able to review chat history when needed.

There are two settings you need to select to enable both those features. The first feature is to enable same-day chats with a particular person to show in the same chat window. This is in the Sametime preferences screen in the **Sametime | Chat Window** settings. The **Save opened chats across sessions** feature should be selected:

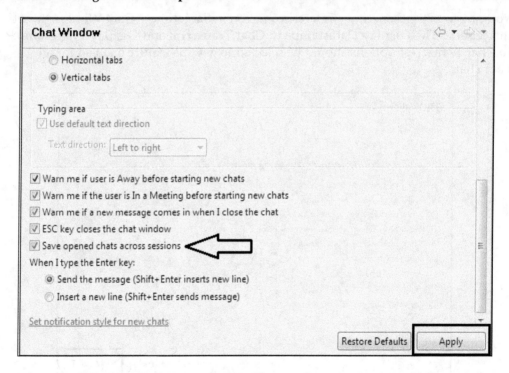

When you open a chat with someone you have chatted with earlier in the day, the previous text will appear in the chat window.

To keep the long-term history of all your chats, you need to go out to the Sametime preferences and select **Sametime | Chat History**:

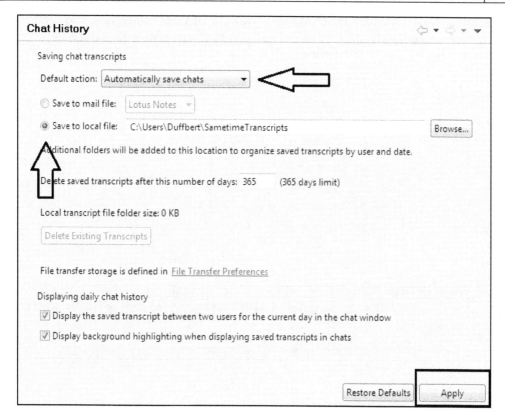

You have various options to set here to fine-tune the settings for saving your chat history. Your default action is set to **Automatically save chats**. You also have the ability to never save chats or to be prompted each time. You can choose to save your chats to your mail file, or to save the chats to a file folder. Note that if you are using the Sametime Connect client you will not have the option to save to your mail file. Chat histories can only be saved locally for the Sametime Connect client. Remember that if you save a file locally it will only be available to the workstation upon which it was saved. If you work in multiple locations you might want to save the chat history to a network file sharing device or server.

From **Chat History** preferences you can also set the number of days that your chats should be saved. At the bottom of the preferences are the options to save and display the daily chats in the current window, as well as shading the chat history so that it's easier to tell what was in a chat prior in the day and what was in part of the current chat.

When you want to display the chat history for one of your colleagues, you can right-click on their name in the contact list. The pop-up menu you see has an option to display the **Chat History**:

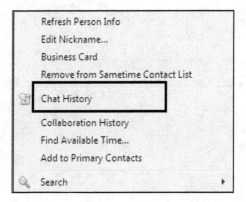

When you select that option, you will see a chat box that lists all the people you've chatted with at the left side, the dates of each chat transcript for the person selected at the top, and chat transcript below:

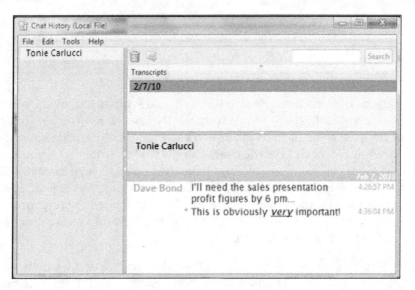

You can now call up any of your saved transcripts and review the activity. One last word about chat transcripts. If your Sametime server allows the creation of chat transcripts you have the option in each chat window of preventing those with whom you are chatting from saving, copying, or printing your chat. If you're uncertain about how your chat might be used you can issue this command at the beginning of your chat dialog. Select **Tools | Prevent Transcript Save**.

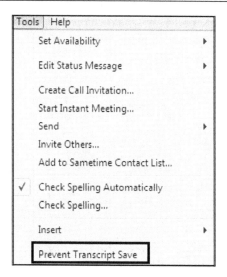

Your chat partner will be aware that you have prevented their ability to save the chat because a new icon will display on the Sametime client—the **Disable Chat Transcript** button.

To disable the **Prevent Transcript Save**, simply deselect it in the **Tools** dialog and the chat transcription can resume.

Spell-checking your chat messages

Sametime helps you avoid typographical errors by providing the ability to spell-check your messages. Perhaps you're corresponding with someone you don't know in person or someone who is a senior manager in your organization. One of the more embarrassing things you can do is to send chat messages that contain typographical errors. Because chat messages tend to be quick and to the point, many people don't bother to re-read the message before they send it.

The first way to implement spell-check is to make the option a permanent part of your configuration. You can select this in your Sametime preferences under the **Sametime | Spell Checking** settings:

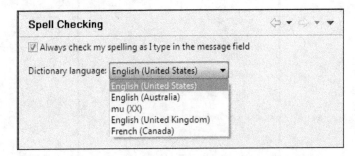

This configures Sametime to check for spelling errors as you type a new message. At this time you can also set your dictionary preference. If your primary language is English, and you are working in the United Kingdom, you may want to select the **English (United Kingdom)** dictionary. This will allow certain words to be bypassed if you use the typically UK spellings.

With this option set, misspelled words will show in your chat area with a red squiggly line under the misspelling:

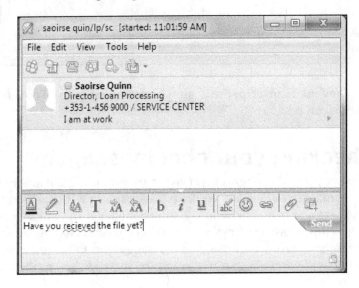

If you choose not to have this option selected, you can still spell check individual messages. If you highlight the message and click the **abc** icon in the toolbar, the same type of spell checking occurs that happened if you had the preference for spell checking set.

Uploading and displaying files, graphics, and web links

It's said that a picture is worth a thousand words. While we're not sure if that's true, we do know that it's faster to send an image than to type 1000 words. Sametime lets you use graphics to convey information, as well as include web links and send files to other colleagues.

Sending files

Let's say you have a file that you need to send to a colleague. If you're both signed on to Sametime, you can do this very quickly. Click the paperclip icon on the toolbar to select the file you want to send. You will get a file selection dialog box that allows you to pick a file from your computer. Once you do that, you will see the file shown in your chat area:

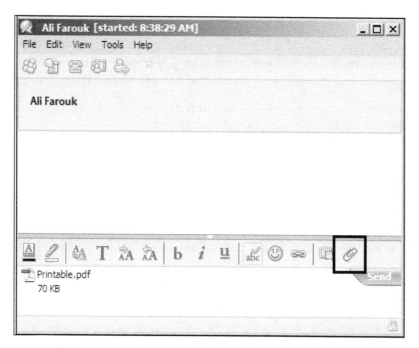

At the sender's end, you'll see the file transfer display in a new box at the bottom of the screen:

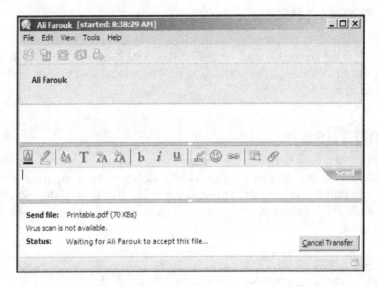

You have the option to cancel the transfer from your end if you need to, but your chat partner will have the option to accept the transfer and start the process.

If you're on the receiving end of a file transfer, then you'll get a similar type of chat window with the option to accept the file being sent:

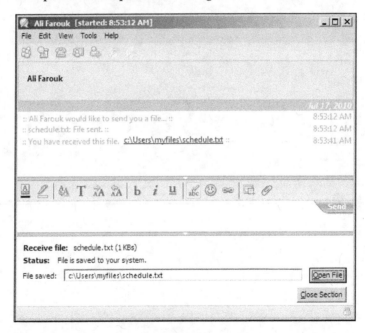

When the transfer is completed, you can open the file directly from the chat window in order to view the results. You can also close the lower section that shows the file transfer. Closing the section doesn't affect the transfer at all after it is finished. It will just make your window smaller.

Your Sametime administrator may have set a maximum file size limit on all files sent via the Sametime chat window. The default maximum is 1 MB, but most administrators do increase this somewhat. Check with your technical staff to confirm the maximum file transfer size.

Some Sametime configurations also exclude certain file types from transfer. These typically include .exe, .bat, and .com files. This is normally done for security reasons as those types of files can contain viruses and other malware. Your company or organization may also have policies about excluding files in general, so be sure to check with your Sametime administrator if this feature appears not to be working for you.

Sending graphics

You can also use Sametime to send graphics to your chat partners. All you need to do is copy the graphic from whatever source you want, and then paste the graphic into the chat area:

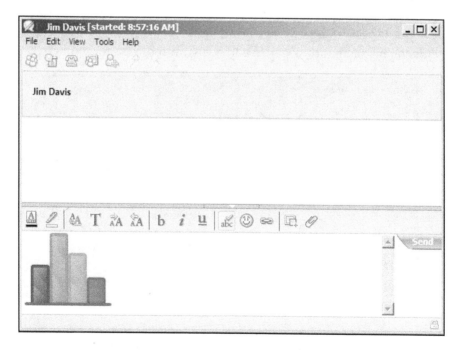

When your chat partner gets the message, they'll see it in the same way you sent it:

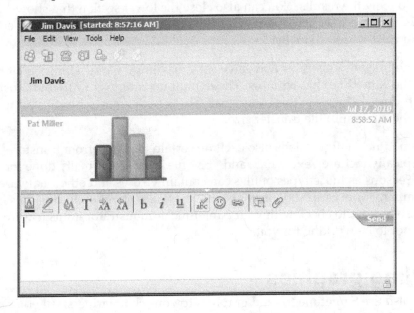

Sending links

Finally, you can also send web addresses, or URLs, to your chat partner. The icon that does that is the one that looks like chain links. When you click that icon, you will get a dialog box that allows you to add a URL and phrase for your chat:

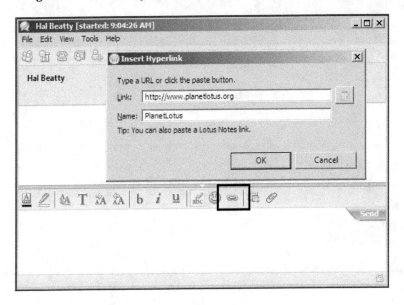

When you click on **OK**, you get a clickable link in your chat window that will go to the address you specified:

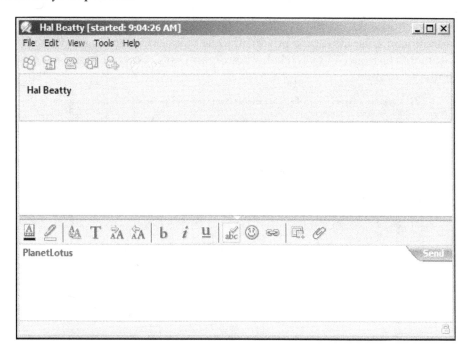

You also have the option to highlight a word in your chat and click the hyperlink icon. You still get the same dialog box that was mentioned before, but now the Name field is pre-populated with the word or phrase that you highlighted.

Sending announcements

Have you ever needed to notify your online team that an "emergency" meeting needs to be held in fifteen minutes? Or perhaps you may need to send a notice to a large group of users that doesn't require a group chat or a response from those users. You can do this by sending a Sametime announcement.

Begin by selecting a name or group of names. Then click the **Send Announcement** button.

The **Send Announcement** dialog will display. You can type in your announcement and modify your recipient list by adding or removing names that are included in the list. Once you've completed the list, click on **Send** to send the announcement. You can also choose the option to allow recipients to respond. A word of caution about announcements; they are a powerful tool. You don't want to send too many announcements as they can overwhelm your teammates or other members of your Sametime community.

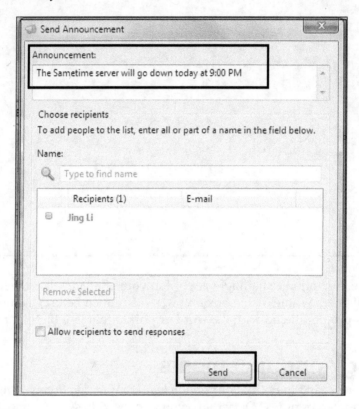

Your announcement will pop up on your recipient's desktop. It might look something like this:

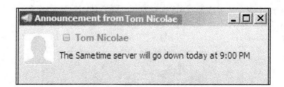

Explain yourself with the screen capture tool

How many times have you been talking or chatting with someone, and you know that showing them your screen (or a part of it) would clarify your discussion completely? Sametime has a great feature called the Screen Capture tool that lets you do just that. You can draw a rectangle around any part of your screen and "capture" it as an image that you can then send to your chat partner. Here's how you do that.

Go to the window or screen that has the information you want to capture with the screen capture tool. Then start a chat with your colleague, making sure the window or screen you want to capture is the first screen underneath your chat window. For the example here, you want to capture the action bar of a Notes application you're using, so you'll position the chat window over the top of your Notes application:

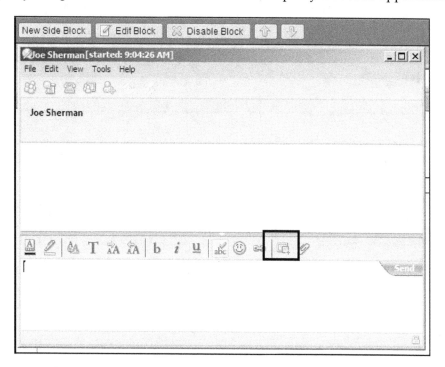

The second to last icon on the chat toolbar next to the paperclip is a pair of rectangles. When you click that icon, your chat window will disappear, and an icon that looks like a plus sign will show up on the screen or window that was underneath your chat window. Position the icon at one of the corners of the area you want to capture, click and hold your mouse button, and drag the selection square to cover the area you want to show to your chat partner.

When you release the mouse button, the area you captured will display as a dialog box in your chat window:

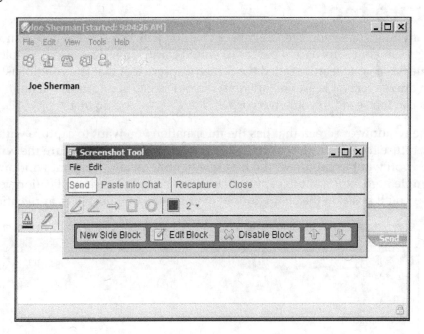

To capture just a section of the screen, you drew a selection box around the action bar of the Notes application, and it was captured for your chat. When you click on **Send**, that image will be sent to your chat partner.

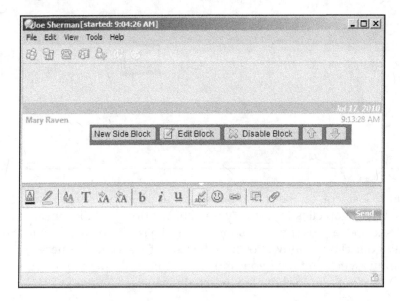

Sometimes a simple screen capture isn't enough to tell your chat partner exactly what you need to convey to them. You may need to annotate the screen capture in some way to point out relevant information. Sametime can do that too. Here's an example of a screen capture box using the annotation tools:

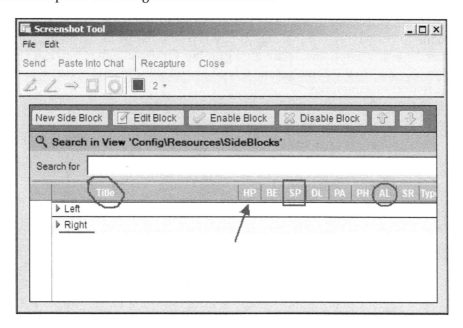

In this example, you've used the icons under the menu line to add to the image. The first pencil icon allows you to draw a freehand line around whatever you'd like. The second pencil icon draws a straight line on the screen. The arrow icon does what you'd expect. It draws an arrow on the screen. The square and circle icons allow you to put squares and circles around an area on your image. Finally, the colored box and the number define what color the line will be, as well as how thick the line is drawn.

Using these simple tools, you can make your chat sessions even more productive, and you can share information quickly and efficiently.

Get emotional with emoticons

As mentioned earlier, it's hard to convey emotion with simple text. You may mean something as a joke, but without body language and verbal clues, your reader may have no way of telling that was the case. Another feature of Sametime that lets you add in some of those textual clues is the use of emoticons.

Emoticons, or "emotion icons" are normally text-based characters that, when used together, stand for a certain emotion. So if you put a colon and a right parenthesis together, it looks like a sideways happy face :). A wink is a semi-colon and a right parenthesis where the lower part of the semi-colon looks like a winking eye ;).

Sametime takes emoticons one step further by substituting animated graphics for those common emoticons. For instance, if you type the happy face icon, Sametime will replace it with a happy face animated graphic. Or if you'd like, you can click on the happy face icon in the Sametime chat toolbar and select from the emoticons that are already part of Sametime:

If you hover over any of the icons with your cursor, a small tip bubble will appear telling you what the emoticon/graphic is conveying in terms of emotion.

Once you start using emoticons, it's almost a certainty that you'll want to add a few of your own to your collection. This means you'll want to call up the emoticon palette and edit the contents. To do that, click the **Edit...** button on the emoticons window to get the emoticon palette preferences screen:

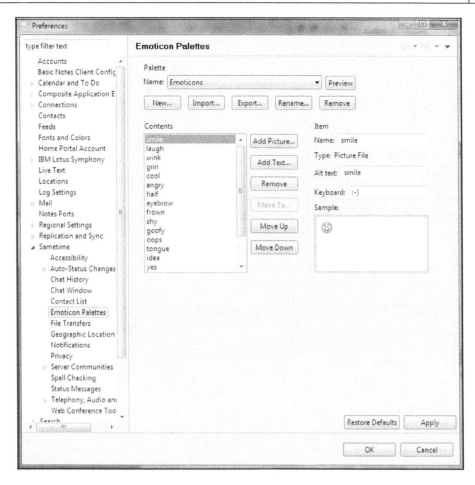

From here, you have a number of options:

- Create a new emoticon palette
- Add a packaged set of emoticons using **Import**
- Share your emoticons with others using **Export**
- Rename your emoticon palette
- Remove the emoticon palette completely using **Delete**
- Add one emoticon to your existing palette by clicking on **Add Picture**
- Add a text emoticon by clicking on **Add Text**
- Remove a single emoticon by clicking on the **Remove** button
- Reorder your emoticons by using the **Move To**, **Move Up**, and **Move Down** buttons

If you find you're not happy with your emoticon palette and you want to start over, clicking on the **Restore Defaults** button will put the standard emoticons back in your palette and get rid of all the additions you've made.

Your colleagues may also send you emoticons in chats that you like and which you can add to your collection. How do you do that? Right click on the emoticon (or Control + click if you're using Sametime on a Mac) and click on **Add to emoticon palette**. If you have multiple collections or palettes you'll need to choose the one to which you want to add the new emoticon, then update the fields to identify the new emoticon and click on **Apply | Ok**.

Your chat palette is stored locally on the workstation. If you work on multiple workstations or work with the Sametime Connect client you may want to export your emoticon palette and import it to your other locations. You can do this by going to **File | Preferences | Sametime | Emoticon Palettes**. Select the name of your emoticon palette and then select **Export**. The **Export Palette** dialog will be displayed and you can select where you want to save this file.

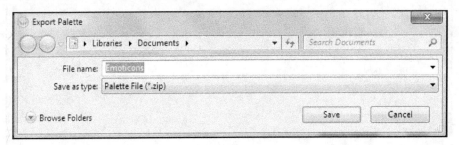

If you are chatting with someone who is using an instant messaging client other than Sametime that may not support graphical icons, your colleague will only see the ASCII or character representation of the emoticon. So while you may have typed the smiley emoticon, they may only see the : -) characters.

Remember that cultural differences may affect how emoticons are interpreted. If you are uncertain about what type of reaction you might receive when you use an emoticon, especially in a business discussion, it might be best to limit the chat to text only!

Audio/video services

If you are connected to a Sametime Standard server, you may be able to take advantage of several audio and video functions to expand chat beyond the chat window. More than just text-based collaboration, with Sametime you can initiate audio, video, and telephone-based communication from within a Sametime chat window.

First things first, you'll need to confirm that you have those features available to you. Check with your Sametime Administrator to be sure that video and audio chats are available for use. Some networks require special tuning for video chatting because they can require additional intranet network resources.

Next you'll need to make sure that you've got the proper gadgetry—do you have sound and video on your workstation? A headset with a microphone is best for sound clarity, but you can also use a stand-alone microphone and speakers. Microphone, headset, or speaker sets may either have USB plugs or separate color-coded plugs to connect to your workstation. If you're not sure about how these should be configured, be sure to contact your IT support staff. You will also require a sound card and USB-connected camera. The camera is a requirement if you plan to do any video chatting and will provide two-way video.

By now you've become familiar with the Sametime preferences dialog box as the central site for making configuration changes to other features of Sametime. We'll begin by checking the **Telephony, Audio and Video** settings. If you do not have access to these types of services or if you are not logged in to Sametime, this option may not appear in the selection list.

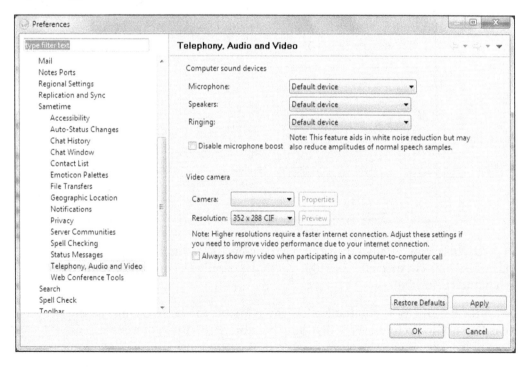

As you see there are settings in this panel for video camera, microphone, speakers, and ring devices.

Voice chatting

With your Sametime audio settings enabled, you can initiate computer-to-computer audio chats or calls with up to five of your colleagues (including yourself). Of course, this all depends on your contacts being audio-enabled as well.

To begin an audio chat, click on the Telephone icon in the Sametime toolbar and choose **Call Selected Contact** or **Create Call Invitation**:

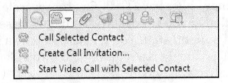

When you receive a call you'll see a screen similar to this:

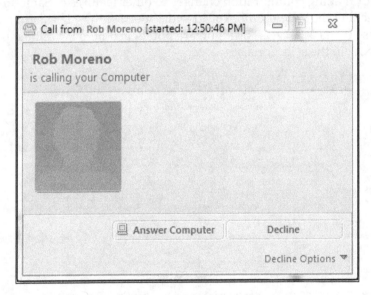

If you decline, you do have the option to convert the call to chat in lieu of taking a voice chat. This is especially useful if you have people in your office and you want the chat to occur later.

Once you start the call, you have a toolbar available to you to change settings regarding audio preferences—including the ability to mute your chat.

Video chatting

So you've started an audio chat. Wouldn't it be nice to see the person with whom you're chatting? You do have the ability to convert a voice chat to a video chat. While audio allows five participants, video only supports chats between yourself and one other person. While this may seem like a limitation, video chatting is really meant to be more for one-on-one video chats. If you need to have more individuals involved in a video conference, then the Sametime Meeting Center (covered in a later chapter) is more appropriate.

To convert your voice chat to video, from the toolbar in the audio chat, click **Start my Video** from the Video Controls icon.

You also have the option to make all your audio calls video-enabled from the **Sametime Preferences | Telephone, Audio and Video | Always show video when making or receiving calls on my computer**.

Telephone to telephone chatting

For telephone to telephone chatting to occur your telephony provider must be integrated with Sametime. You must also have the telephone number for your Sametime contact. Some telephony systems allow you to have several locations, for example Office or Home Office, so from the Telephone icon you will need to select your preferred device, then select one of your contacts and click on the telephone icon.

Audio, video, and telephone to telephone chats are a wonderful feature of Sametime, but may take some assistance from your local IT staff to get you up to speed. Additionally, keep in mind that if you are working over video across wide area networks, there may be some video lag issues. Finally, if you notice that you are in a chat and some options are grayed out or not available for use, this may be due to the one of the other participants using an older version of the Sametime client. This may also occur if you are including colleagues who are connected to a Sametime server community other than your own. Be sure to check with your Sametime Administrator if you have questions.

Integrating Sametime with Microsoft Office, Microsoft Outlook, and Microsoft SharePoint

It is possible to take advantage of many of the collaborative features of Sametime even if you're running Sametime with Microsoft Outlook, Microsoft Office, or Microsoft SharePoint. With the use of Sametime plug-ins, presence awareness, instant messaging, and web conferencing can be made available in all three of these tools. If the plug-ins are enabled, you will see the familiar Sametime availability icons next to usernames. By clicking on those icons, you can start a chat or a web conference just like you would from within Lotus Notes using the Sametime Embedded client or from within the Sametime Connect client.

In Microsoft Outlook, for example, icons will be added to the Outlook toolbar. This allows you to search for contacts, open your Sametime contact list, start a chat, video or voice chat, or join a Sametime meeting. You can also see the Sametime awareness status of an e-mail sender! So if you prefer Outlook for e-mail, you can still take advantage of some Sametime Embedded functionality.

The installation of Sametime integration plug-ins is dependent on many variables, including what version of the Sametime client you're running, as well as what has been installed on the Microsoft Office and Microsoft SharePoint installations. It is best to work with your technical staff to make sure that you have all the required elements in place.

Your Sametime administrator may also have packaged the integration of the plug-ins to your Sametime Connect client install. In most cases the plug-ins are packaged in a `.jar` format and are added as you would with any other Sametime plug-in.

For more information on how this is done, see here: `http://publib.boulder.ibm.com/infocenter/sametime/v8r0/index.jsp?topic=/com.ibm.help.sametime.802.doc/Standard/st_inst_installingsametimeintegrationwms_t.html`

Summary

In this chapter, you learned how Sametime chat sessions are encrypted for privacy. You learned how to change the font styling of your messages to communicate more effectively, how to keep track of the date and time of your instant messages, and how to save transcripts of your chats for future reference. You learned how Sametime can automatically spell-check your instant messages and how you can share files, graphics, and web links in an instant message. You also learned how you can capture portions of your screen, annotate the images, and send them to your chat partner. You learned about emoticons and why they can be helpful in your chats. You then learned how to use them effectively, save new emoticons, and how to share your emoticon palettes with others. You learned how Sametime can be used to have voice and video chats to supplement your text chats. And finally, you learned how Sametime can also integrate with Microsoft Office, Outlook, and SharePoint to allow these to access the power of Sametime within those software tools.

6
Spread the Word: Connecting to other Messaging Communities

You've now been using Sametime in your organization to communicate and collaborate more effectively. You're sending instant messages rich in information, including files and graphics. You're even able to initiate and use video and voice chats when the situation calls for it. In short, you're a Sametime power user!

What else can you do to extend the power of Sametime? In our ever-increasing global environment you may need or want to chat and communicate with people outside of your organization. These people could be Sametime users in other companies, or they may be users of one of the various instant messaging applications, such as Google Talk, Yahoo Instant Messenger, or AOL Instant Messenger. Is there any way you can communicate with those individuals without having to manage multiple instant messaging clients? Yes! Sametime has a feature called the Sametime Gateway that, if installed, allows you to communicate with other instant messaging applications from within your Sametime client.

In this chapter, you'll learn how to:

- Connect to a local Sametime community
- Connect to and communicate with an external Sametime community
- Connect to and communicate with other instant messaging services, such as AOL Instant Messaging, Yahoo Instant Messaging, and Google Talk
- Use different Sametime directory types: Domino versus LDAP

Connect to your local Sametime community

The most basic use of Sametime is to communicate with members of your local Sametime community. Typically "local" refers to the primary Sametime server that your organization uses on a regular basis. As we've shown you previously, many of the settings regarding Sametime can be set via the Preferences dialog. Sametime community settings are no exception.

Before we begin it is important to realize that depending on how your Sametime administrators have configured your environment, you may only be able to access your local or primary Sametime community. Due to regulatory or security reasons, you may be prevented from accessing external Sametime communities as well as non-Sametime instant messaging applications. For example:

- Babak would like to use Sametime to connect and chat with some of his colleagues at another university regarding some upcoming research meetings. He has confirmed that both universities use Sametime.

- Danila is working on a project with some individuals who are outside of her company. She knows they have gmail addresses. Can she chat with them via Sametime?

- Laurel has several teammates who are getting ready to travel to other countries to work on long-term projects. She'd like to stay in touch with them. Her teammates will be working for a company that uses a Jabber server for instant messaging.

- Mike has several children in college. The company that he works for is very family-oriented, and allows employees to maintain contact with their families via instant messaging.

You are now ready to get started expanding your Sametime contact list to include external contacts. If you are using the Sametime Embedded client, your Lotus Notes and Sametime administrators may have preconfigured your Lotus Notes installation so that your Sametime community was already listed for you. We'll assume that this has not been done and we'll show you how to add a new community.

Let's begin by signing on to Sametime using the **Log In to Sametime** dialog box. You should enter your Sametime host server name (check with your Sametime administrator if you don't know the name of the server) and your username and password. To set up your Sametime community information, click on the **Connectivity** button which will take you to an additional set of screens that show all the details of your connection to the Sametime server. You can also find this same dialog information from your Sametime preferences under the **Server Communities** settings.

The **Server community name** is a name you give your community to distinguish it from other communities you may be part of. It can be any name, and is often the name of the Sametime server or the organization that is running the Sametime server.

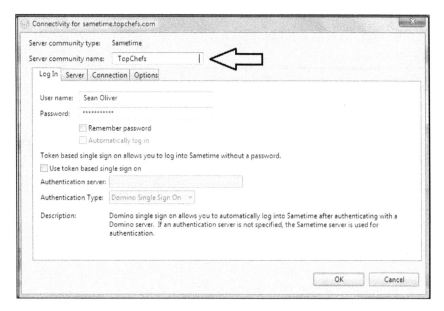

The **Log In** tab configures your personal identification information for this particular Sametime server. It carries over the information from the sign-on screen where applicable, if that's how you accessed this screen. If you are using Single Sign-on as described in *Chapter 2*, you can specify your information on this tab. Single Sign-on allows you to only have to login once—whether it is from your Notes client or your Windows central login.

It's a good idea to check with your Sametime administrator before you make changes to this screen. They will advise you regarding which options to choose if Single Sign-on is an option for your environment. Domino Single Sign-on uses a secret key that is passed to your Domino server so that when you login to your Notes client you are logged into Sametime as well.

The next tab to review is the **Server** tab. This stores the name of the Sametime server, along with what port the Sametime server is using to communicate with Sametime clients. Port 1533 is the common default port used when Sametime is installed, but check with your Sametime administrator to make sure that it is correct. The **Send Keep Alive Signal regular font** allows your Sametime client to check the server every 60 seconds to make sure you are still connected, and to notify you on a timely basis if you are disconnected for any reason.

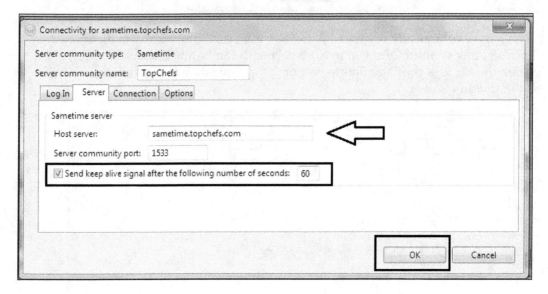

The **Connection** tab configures the type of network connection to be used when your Sametime client is communicating with the server. As the screen directs, you should not change this setting unless your Sametime administrator directs you to do so.

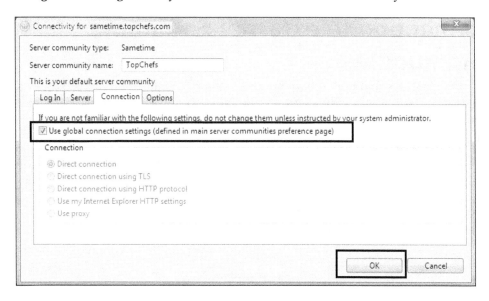

Finally, the **Options** tab determines if this server will show any awareness information for people who are signed on to this server. It also sets whether you can use a common name format, such as "Jane Smith", or whether you have to use the entire name format as it is stored on the server, such as "CN=Jane Smith/ OU=Accounting/O=Acme". This is known as a canonical format, where CN stands for "common name", OU stands for "organizational unit", and O stands for "organization".

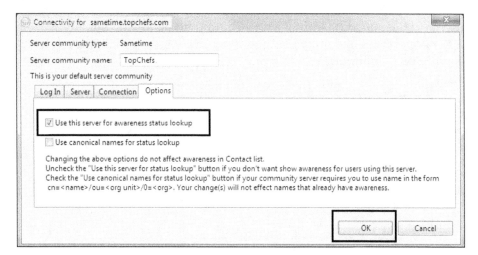

Once you click on **OK**, this information is stored as your preference and will be used whenever you sign on to Sametime using this community.

Connecting to external Sametime communities

One of the features that makes Sametime so powerful is the ability to be connected with external Sametime communities while also being logged into your internal community. Imagine the power of being connected to various organizations you do business with and having the ability to collaborate instantly.

Setting up an external community in Sametime is nearly identical to setting up an internal community. Clicking on the drop-down arrow on the **Sametime Contacts** bar will give you the option to set up a new Sametime Community:

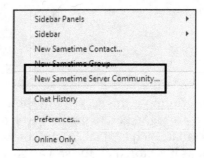

When you click on that option, you're presented with a dialog box that is nearly identical to the dialog box you get when you set up your internal Sametime community.

You also have the option of adding a new community if you are already working within the Preferences dialog by going to Sametime communities and selecting **Add New Server Community**.

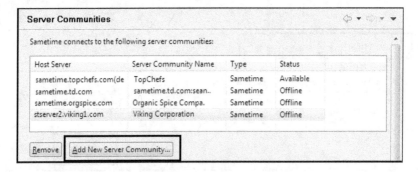

If you have external Sametime communities added, you'll be able to see and manage them from your Sametime preferences under the **Server Communities** option:

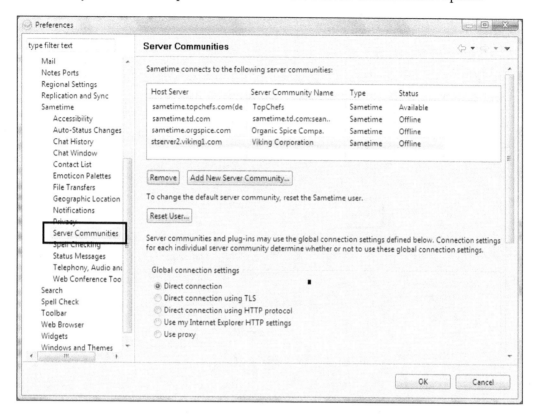

If you need to remove a Sametime community if it is no longer relevant or accessible, select the community and click on the **Remove** button. Be warned! This will remove your groups and contacts associated with this community, so be sure that you want to proceed, as there is no undo button!

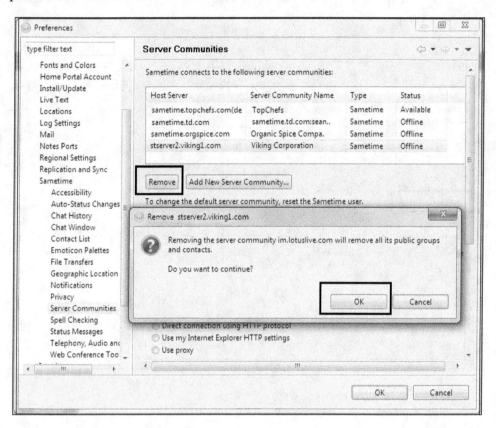

Each of your Sametime communities will show up as separate icons under the **Sametime Contacts** title bar. If your cursor hovers over any one of the status icons, you'll see a pop-up message that tells you which community the icon represents, along with your current status message for that community:

If you click on the drop-down arrow next to any of the community icons or the **All** option, you will see the options you have available to you:

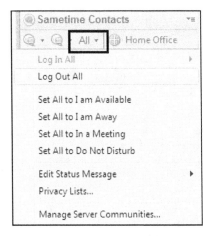

You can log into or out of your Sametime community, set status messages, edit status messages, or set the privacy options for each community. If you click on the drop-down for the **All** option, you can log into or out of all the Sametime communities at once, as well as setting your status message for all communities at the same time.

Connecting to other instant messaging users: AOL, Google, and Yahoo

There's a third type of connection you can make in your Sametime client, which is a connection to public instant messaging networks like AOL, Google, and Yahoo. From within your Sametime client, not only can you be connected to people within your organization, but you can be connected to other individuals regardless of whether they use Sametime or not.

The ability to make this type of connection is based on a Sametime server feature called the Sametime Gateway. The Sametime Gateway allows for communication between Sametime and other instant messaging networks. Some organizations may choose not to enable this feature, as the encryption of your Sametime communication cannot be maintained when you connect with the other instant messaging applications. Therefore, security or regulatory concerns may prevent you from being able to use this feature.

If your organization is running the Sametime Gateway, you will notice a slightly different dialog box when you attempt to add a new Sametime Contact. You are given the option to add a new contact by their e-mail address and then specify which instant messaging provider that Sametime should look to for the connection:

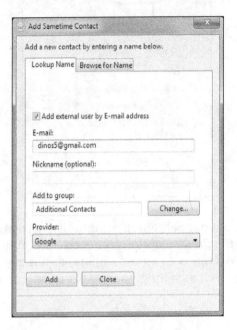

The provider options are listed in the drop-down field:

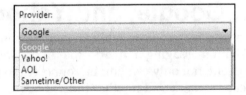

Google, **Yahoo!**, and **AOL** options are well-known. The **Sametime/Other** option is designed to allow you to connect to other instant messaging communities that use the Extensible Messaging and Presence Protocol, also known as XMPP. Jabber is one example of an XMPP-based network. Your Sametime administrator can work with you to determine if an instant messaging network that's not specifically listed supports the XMPP protocol, as well as whether you can connect your Sametime client to that network.

To add your contacts, you'll need to know what external network they use, and the e-mail address they use on those systems. Just as you did previously, click on the **New** contact button.

Select the **Add external user by E-mail address** option. Type in your contact's e-mail address and select a provider from the **Provider** drop-down list. Be sure that your contact's e-mail address matches the provider you select. For example, if their e-mail address ends in "gmail.com", select Google. Once you click on **Add**, the dialog box will display the e-mail address of the chat contact that was added to your Sametime group.

One thing to keep in mind here is that once you have added your contact, their status may not immediately display as active in your contact list. Other instant messaging applications often give your contact the chance to approve or reject the invitation to be added to their contact list. If your chat partner rejects your invitation, you will not see them as active, nor will you be able to chat with them. Conversely, if they accept the invitation, they will show as active in your contact list, using the awareness icons of the service they belong to, as shown in the following screenshot:

Once that is completed, you can chat with them just as if they are another Sametime user:

One thing to notice is that most of the special features of Sametime chatting, such as sharing graphics, screen captures, or using special text formatting are disabled for chats with contacts on other platforms. Since Sametime cannot guarantee that the chat client of your contact has the same type of features that you have, it simply disables those features that may not work on your contact's chat client. You can tell which options will work as they will still be active and not grayed out in the toolbar. Sametime communities may also not be configured in the same way and features may be disabled or hidden based on corporate or organizational policies. The administrator of the Sametime Gateway has the ability to set whether your online presence or even the ability to chat with external networks like Yahoo and Google is enabled. As we've said before, when in doubt about the availability of a feature—contact your Sametime administrator.

This is an example of contacts being added to all three chat providers, as well as the awareness icons they use when the contact is signed on and available.

Directory types: Domino versus LDAP

While we're discussing Sametime communities, we want to mention briefly the differences you may see between Sametime directory lookups. Sametime administrators have the option of configuring Sametime to use either the Lotus Domino directory, which is the central directory for Lotus Notes users, or a Lightweight Directory Access Protocol, or LDAP, directory. Why is this important to you? Because you may have different options for directory look ups from one type to the other.

In a Domino Directory environment, Sametime uses names as they are configured for Lotus Notes users. This is typically displayed in a format Lotus Notes users see in e-mails that includes some information about the person, such as their department or organization. The name may display something like: Alise Brown/Accounting/TOPCHEFS. When searching the directory, you will see the Domino Directory related information. Check with your Sametime administrator if you can't see the **Browse for Name** tab, as this option may be turned off in your environment.

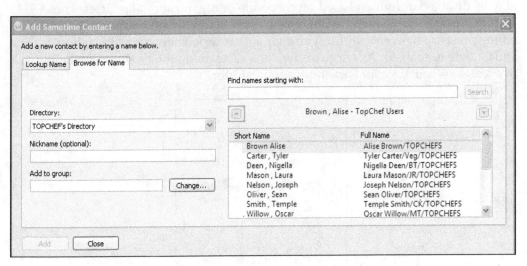

An LDAP configured environment may only display the short name or abbreviated name of a user. You could also see that the directory has names that are displayed in LDAP format such as cn=alise brown, ou=accounting, dc=topchefs, dc=org. This is helpful to know when you are searching for a name, as you may only be able to search for the name in its abbreviated format like "abrown" or "Alise Brown". The Domino or LDAP directory searches only affect those contacts that are connected to other Sametime communities, and not to external networks like Google or AOL. Check with your Sametime administrator if you have questions!

Summary

In this chapter, you learned how to join an internal Sametime community as well as how to join external Sametime communities. You learned how all these communities can be logged into at the same time, so that you can chat with both internal and external contacts seamlessly. You also learned how to tell if your Sametime environment is running the Sametime Gateway software, and if so, how to add contacts from public instant messaging platforms such as AOL, Yahoo, and Google. Finally, you learned how searching for users may be affected by using a Domino directory or an LDAP directory.

7
iNotes and Sametime—
Chatting from the Web

Up to this chapter, the assumption has been that you are sitting at your own computer and that you have Sametime installed on that specific desktop or laptop. But in today's world of wireless connectivity, multiple computers, internet cafés, and so on, is that completely realistic? What if your laptop crashes while you're visiting the branch office in another country, and it'll be two weeks before you can get back and get your laptop fixed? Can Sametime adapt to a worst-case scenario such as that?

Well, of course! If you're running the web version of the Notes e-mail system known as iNotes, you can easily have Sametime up and running just by signing on to your e-mail though a web browser. If you're used to running the embedded version of Sametime in the Notes client, you'll hardly be able to tell the difference.

In this chapter, you'll learn how to:

- Set the Sametime preference in iNotes
- Log into Sametime from iNotes
- Chat with others using Sametime from iNotes
- Display Sametime contacts in the iNotes sidebar
- Add new contacts to Sametime in iNotes
- Set and change your availability status in Sametime for iNotes
- Launch the Help files for Sametime in iNotes

Using Sametime in iNotes

Let's talk a little bit about iNotes. iNotes is the Lotus Notes web client. It works with browsers like Microsoft Internet Explorer, Mozilla Firefox, and Apple Safari. To get started using iNotes, you will need to login with a user ID and password that your e-mail administrator has given you. Your company or organization may have a central website for you to use to login, like webmail.companyname.com, so that the login URL is easy to remember. Some possible uses for iNotes and Sametime include:

- Beza uses a netbook and doesn't want to install either the Notes client or Sametime Connect client. Sametime in iNotes allows him to contact his friends and colleagues.

- Maja primarily works from a kiosk. She can use iNotes and Sametime to access her e-mail and her company's directory.

- Tatiana is traveling without her laptop. She'd like to connect with her team members. She's stopped at an internet café where she's able to login to iNotes and Sametime.

When you first login to iNotes you should see your inbox displayed. iNotes has several modes: Full Mode, Lite Mode, and Ultralite Mode. Each of these modes has specific features. We're going to focus on Full Mode as that is the version that allows you to login to Sametime. The following figure shows an iNotes Mail inbox. If you are using the Home tab or Welcome page as it was previously called, your opening page may display a slightly different view when you open iNotes.

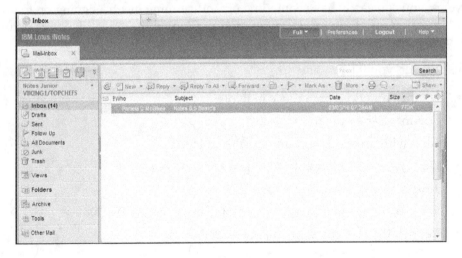

If you're used to using Notes as your e-mail client, you'll notice a very strong similarity to the Notes 8.x mail client, so you should already be pretty comfortable with the display on the screen.

Enable instant messaging

Because you are using Sametime in a web browser, there are far fewer preferences that are available to you. This is because, in a web browser, you don't have the ability to control a rich Sametime client as you do when you're running within the Sametime Connect client. The web browser version of Sametime is meant to deliver a basic set of functionality that works regardless of what type of computer you're using.

The first thing you need to make sure of is that Sametime is enabled to run within iNotes. You do this by launching the iNotes preferences in the upper-right corner of your browser window:

When you click on the **Preferences** option, you'll see a list of iNotes preferences, one of which allows you to enable Instant Messaging.

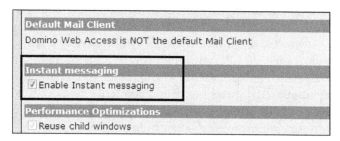

After you select the **Enable Instant messaging** option, click on **Save** and **Close**. This saves the preference in your iNotes profile. At this point your screen will refresh and you'll notice a new twisty icon just below the toolbar above your name in the inbox.

In order to get Sametime started, click on the twisty icon and highlight the option to **Log On To Instant Messaging**. Once you're logged in you'll notice your awareness changes to **Available**.

If you have never launched Sametime in iNotes before, the browser has to load a Java application called STLinksApp to allow Sametime to work properly. You'll see the following warning box, and you click on **Run** to let the browser load the application and launch Sametime.

Be sure to select **Always trust content from this publisher** and **Run**. The wording for these options may vary slightly with the browser you are using. It is very important that you select this application to run. Some of the functionality we describe later may not work if it has not been installed. Check with your systems staff regarding your default browser settings and whether or not you have the system authority to run these types of Java applets.

Chatting from iNotes

Now that you've logged into Sametime, you may notice that your contacts are showing their Sametime status in the iNotes inbox. Do you want to start a chat with one of them? You've got several methods for doing just that.

The first option you have is to right-click on an e-mail that shows online awareness for a contact. When you do so, a drop-down menu appears as shown in the following screenshot:

Select the **Chat with...** option. Once you do that, a new chat window will appear. From the same menu you can also select **Add to Sametime Contact List**. This allows you to add the person to your Sametime Contact list. Remember, this list is stored on the server, so if you use Sametime elsewhere your contacts will follow you!

Another option to start a chat is by choosing the Sametime conversation icon in the iNotes toolbar and selecting **Chat with** from the pull-down dialog box. This same dialog also allows you to **Add to the Sametime Contact List...** or **Show Sametime Contact List**.

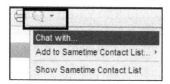

When you begin a chat a new chat window pops up. Be sure that your browser has been configured to support pop-up browser windows, or the chat window may end up being blocked. The window will look something like this:

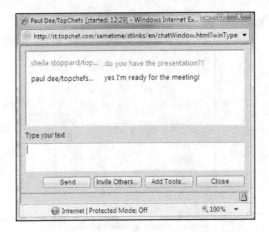

As you see, the chat window in iNotes doesn't look quite the same as the chat window in the Sametime Connect or Sametime Embedded client. One important item to note is that the chat window doesn't have the same toolbar that you've been used to seeing. It does however show the encrypted icon, so the chat conversation is encrypted. The rich text features that you are used to seeing in the Sametime Embedded client and the Sametime Connect client aren't available either. So you can't change fonts or include graphic items. You can invite others to the chat, so you can hold a group chat. However, you cannot hold a voice or video chat through Sametime iNotes. If your colleagues send you emoticons they will be converted to the text versions of the standard emoticon set. Because you're working in a browser environment, it is probably a good idea to keep your conversations short and to the point, as you don't want to time out of your browser session. If this happens frequently, check with your Domino and Sametime administrators.

If screen sharing and whiteboarding are configured for your Sametime server you'll see the **Add Tools** button. Clicking the **Add Tools** button allows you to start a screen sharing or a whiteboarding session in your browser.

If you select either of those options, you will be taken to a new web page that allows you to share your web browser screen or access the whiteboard function in the Sametime Meeting Room.

Displaying Sametime contacts in the sidebar

A new feature of iNotes 8.5.x is the iNotes sidebar. The sidebar panels allow you to customize your iNotes environment to look more like your Notes client environment. You can change your preview pane settings, add your **Day-At-A-Glance** appointments, view **Help** or view your **Sametime Contacts**. To do that, click on the **Show** option drop-down arrow on the far right side of the browser window. This gives you a menu of options, one of which is to open the **Sidebar Panels** and to make sure **Sametime Contacts** is one of the displayed panels.

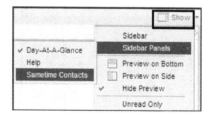

When the application finishes loading, the Sidebar is opened, and the selected panels are displayed. Since you selected **Sametime Contacts** as one of your options, it now appears very much like a Sidebar gadget in the Notes 8.x client. Your Sametime contact list with your groups and contacts will be displayed.

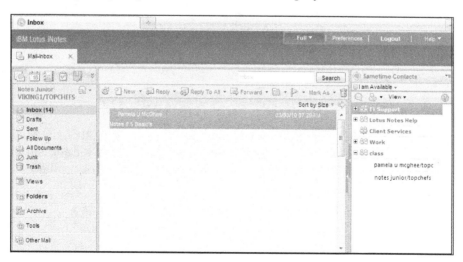

You can also open the sidebar from the Sametime Log on button by selecting **Show Sametime Contact List**. This will display the Sametime contact list in the sidebar.

Clicking on the icons in the Sametime header bar shows various drop-down menus for you to use in setting display preferences, adding contacts, adding groups, and starting chats.

Adding and managing contacts

Adding contacts in iNotes Sametime is just about as easy as adding them in any other version. When you click on the Person icon drop-down arrow, you see a menu that allows you to add a contact, a private group, or a public group to your contact list.

If you right-click on a name in the Sametime sidebar, you'll get a different menu of options allowing you to edit the person's nickname, start a chat, send an e-mail message, configure your display preferences, or even remove the person's name from your Sametime list.

Clicking on the option to add a person gives you a new browser window that allows you to either enter the name manually if you know it or to call up a directory listing so that you can choose a name. To choose a name from the directory list, click on the **Name** button.

The **Name** button brings up a directory dialog browser screen that is similar to what you've seen before. Enter the name of the person to search for and click **Search**. This returns a list of names that match your search criteria. Click the name that you want to add and click on the **Select** button to move it into the Recipients list. When your list is done, click on the **OK** button.

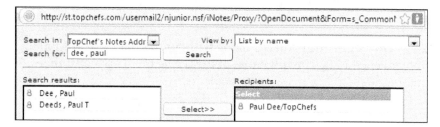

The name populates your original Add Contact window, and you click on **OK** to add it to your contact list permanently.

You can also add the person to the Sametime contact list by right-clicking on their name in your inbox. This will give you the dialog box and option to add them to the Sametime contact list.

One set of options revolve around how your Sametime sidebar panel will display information. If you click on the **View** option drop-down arrow, you will see a number of options that are designed to be turned on or off. To turn the option on, click the option and a checkmark will appear next to it. To turn it off, click it again and the checkmark will disappear.

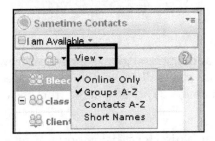

Online Only shows you just the names of people who are signed on to Sametime at the present time. Leaving this turned off means that all your contacts will appear.

Groups A-Z and **Contacts A-Z** will alphabetize your Sametime groups and contacts within the groups. If you turn the option off, the names and groups will appear in the order in which they were added.

Short Names only show the contact's name without the full organizational information attached to it. The full name of the contact will appear if this option is deselected.

Set and edit your status message

You have the ability to display and edit your status messages in the same way you do with other versions of Sametime. You find this option setting on the left side of your iNotes screen, next to the name of the person who is signed on to this account. If you click on the drop-down arrow next to the Sametime availability icon, you see the options to set **Available**, **Away**, **Meeting**, and **Do Not Disturb** options, as well as editing the message to display something more detailed.

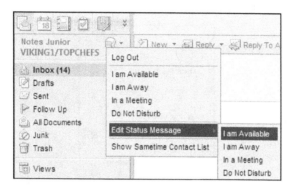

You can also modify your status from the Sametime sidebar. Click on the drop-down arrow next to your status indicator in the sidebar. This will also give you the option to change your status.

When you choose to edit one of your status messages instead of just using the default status message, you will see a window giving you the option to customize the information shown for your status.

Help! I need somebody!

There's a good chance that regardless of how much we put in this book, you'll have that one question that we didn't think to cover. At that point, you should consult the Help system that comes built into Sametime.

On the Sametime panel, you'll see a question mark icon on the right side of the icon bar. After you click on that icon an additional panel launches in the sidebar that has all the help files for iNotes.

If the first topic that comes up is not for **Instant Messaging**, click on the third icon in the icon bar, the one right after the right-facing green arrow. That gives you a list of topics, one of which is for Sametime Help. You should be able to find the answers to most of your questions there.

Summary

In this chapter, you learned how to start Sametime in iNotes. You learned how to start a chat session as well as how to set and change your availability status messages. You learned how to add contacts as well as set the different preferences that you have available in the Sametime iNotes client. Finally, you learned how to launch the Sametime Help files in the iNotes client.

8

Going Mobile—Installing and Using the Sametime Mobile Client

Many of us have at least one mobile device. Because we frequently work away from our desks and use our mobile devices as portable offices, Sametime Instant Messaging is designed to go with you. With the Sametime Mobile client your mobile device becomes an extension of your Sametime contact list and allows you to stay in touch with your contacts wherever you are!

- Lisa is waiting on some information from a team member for a project deadline, but she's away from her desk. However, she has Sametime Mobile installed on her Windows Mobile 6 device and she can connect during her board meeting.

- Juan is on a long distance trip between countries. He doesn't want to pull his laptop down from the overhead bins, but he does have his Blackberry available to chat with his staff in the home office since he has Sametime Mobile installed. He can set his presence awareness to unavailable once he's in the air.

- Logan needs some contract information during a lengthy meeting. He can ping his project team for any detail clarification from his Blackberry using Sametime Mobile, without disrupting the meeting.

In this chapter, you'll learn how to:

- Distinguish between the different options for using Sametime Mobile on devices including Blackberry, Nokia, Sony Ericsson, and Windows Mobile handhelds.
- Work with the different packaging options for downloading the Sametime Mobile software to your mobile device.
- Begin downloading the Sametime Mobile client.
- Use the Sametime Mobile client.
- Initiate a chat with Sametime Mobile.
- Adjust your Sametime Mobile client preferences.
- Manage your Sametime contacts with Sametime Mobile.
- Secure your Sametime Mobile client.

Supported devices for Sametime Mobile

Sametime Mobile is available for a number of mobile operating systems and devices. Devices include those that support the Microsoft Windows Mobile operating system, Research in Motion Blackberry devices, Sony Ericsson cell phones, and Nokia Eseries devices.

As new devices are made available on a continual basis, check both your mobile device website as well as the IBM Sametime support site (`http://www-01.ibm.com/support/docview.wss?rs=477&uid=swg27013765`) for updated information about which devices are supported. Research in Motion provides downloads for Sametime for new devices from their website at `http://www.blackberry.com`.

Device Operating System	Mobile model
Windows Mobile	Windows Mobile 2003 Second Edition Pocket PC
	Windows Mobile 5 Pocket PC
	Windows Mobile Smartphone
	Windows Mobile 6 Standard
	Windows Mobile 6 Professional

Device Operating System	Mobile model
Research in Motion Blackberry	Blackberry 7100
	Blackberry 8100
	Blackberry 8300
	Blackberry 8700
	Blackberry 8800
	Blackberry 8900
	Blackberry 9000
Sony Ericsson	M600i
	P990i
	P1i
Nokia	Eseries

Packaging the Sametime Mobile client for download

As part of the Sametime server installation, files for each of the mobile platforms are included in subdirectories on your organization's Sametime server. Your Sametime administrator makes these files available to you via configuration options. These files will have specific file extensions based on what type of device you have. For example, the files for Sametime Mobile on the Windows Mobile operating system are packaged as a `.cab` file, while `.cod` and `.alx` files are part of the Blackberry download package. Your Sametime administrator will also provide you with a website that will provide access to the files.

Downloading and installing Sametime Mobile

To begin using Sametime Mobile, you must first download and install the application to your mobile device. The installation steps will be specific to the type of device you are using. The process first begins with accessing the download website provided to you by your Sametime administrator. Depending on your device you might use Internet Explorer (Windows Mobile), a browser for mobile phones like Opera, or the Blackberry browser specifically designed for the Blackberry. The URL will be similar to the following: `http://sametime.topchefs.com/mobile/`. When the main download page appears, it will look much like the following screenshot:

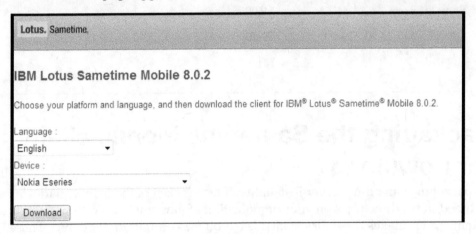

You'll need to select your language and the device type and then select **Download**. You may be prompted for a user ID and password at this point. Your Sametime administrator should provide you with this information. Our example here shows a login screen for a Windows Mobile device:

If your organization or company uses a Blackberry Enterprise Server, they may have configured the server to deploy the Sametime client "over the air" to your device. This means that the Sametime client application may be pushed to your device without any interaction on your part, because the Blackberry Enterprise Server can push out software updates. You can also download the Sametime client from the Blackberry website at `http://na.blackberry.com/eng/services/server/domino/lotus_software.jsp#tab_tab_sametime`. This method uses the Blackberry desktop manager to upload the Sametime client to your Blackberry device using the combination of `.cod` and `.alx` files provided in the install packages. Your Sametime administrator will provide you with a user ID and password for use to login to your organization's Sametime server.

The installation of Sametime Mobile for Windows Mobile includes a couple of extra steps. This installation includes a configuration file that must be downloaded to the device. You should check with your Sametime administrator for additional information if you have questions in this situation.

Using the Sametime Mobile client

So you've downloaded the Sametime Mobile client to your mobile device. Let's confirm that you have installed the application and that you can login and start the application successfully! On the following pages we'll use a Blackberry 8900 or a Windows Mobile 6 device as our working models for the Sametime Mobile images. We're going to cover a number of options and features and they may display somewhat differently depending on the device you use. So as we're going through these options, try to focus more on the function that's being shown rather than the specifics of what is being displayed on the screen.

- Microsoft® Windows® Mobile: Choose **Start** | **Programs** | **Sametime**.
- BlackBerry: Open the **Instant Messaging** folder; choose the **Enterprise Messaging or Sametime** application.
- Nokia: Open the **Installations** folder, choose the **Sametime** application.
- Sony Ericsson: Open the **Tools** folder, choose the **Sametime** application.

Your Blackberry device will show an icon that looks similar to the following screenshot:

The Windows Mobile Device Sametime icon will be similar to the following screenshot:

Logging into Sametime Mobile

To login to Sametime, enter the Sametime user ID and password that your Sametime administrator has provided to you. This would be most likely the user ID and password that you use with the Sametime Embedded client or the Sametime Connect client. You have the ability to save the password and will automatically login the next time you open Sametime on your device. Please note, while it is more convenient to have the device remember your password here, make sure to consult the security policies of your organization when saving a password to a mobile device. Always set a device password for your mobile device, so that in the event that the device is stolen or lost, your accounts and data can't be accessed. The following depicts the login screen for the Sametime client on a Blackberry device:

As we explained earlier, we're going to show screens from both a Blackberry and a Windows Mobile device. We assume that you are familiar with navigating to menu options as one of those device users.

Beginning a chat

When you login, you'll see a list of all your active chats, as well as your contact list groups. You can click on any group name in order to expand it to see the names of the people you have in that group.

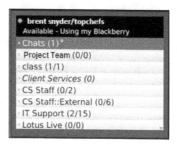

To begin chatting with a contact, move your device cursor and select their name. A blank chat window will appear with a panel for you to begin typing. Your chat conversation will appear in the chat window.

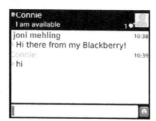

Within the Sametime Mobile client itself, there are option menus to view your contact list, groups, etc. In this example the Blackberry has a pop-up menu that lets you accomplish a number of tasks such as adding a new contact or sending a message to someone.

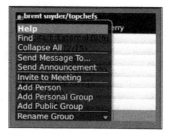

As we've discussed in earlier chapters, emoticons help to convey emotion and "body language" in text messages that could be misread without any verbal or body language context. In Sametime Mobile you still have that feature available to you.

When you're chatting with someone, you will see a small smiley icon to the right of your chat input field (if you're on a Blackberry) or an **Insert Emoticon** option. Sametime Mobile displays a screen of available emoticons that you can click on to insert into your chat message. (See the Blackberry version in the following screenshot.)

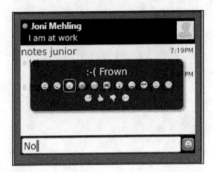

As with the Sametime Embedded or Sametime Connect client, you can invite other contacts to join an ongoing chat. "**Invite Other to Chat**" or "**Invite Others**" will display as a menu option depending on your mobile device. This will display a list of your contacts and you can select one or more names to invite to your current chat.

Sending an announcement

Have you ever wanted to "ping" a number of contacts at one time to let them know of a meeting room change? From the Sametime Mobile client you can send an announcement to all members of a group or choose individual contacts from the group list. This appears on their chat window as an announcement. If you need an easy method to notify a group of users, this is it!

Multiple chat conversations

Another feature that extends to the Sametime Mobile client is the ability to have multiple chat conversations at one time. Regardless of whether you're in front of your computer or on your phone, people are not going to wait for you to finish one chat before you answer theirs. With your Blackberry, Windows Mobile, Sony, or Nokia phone, you'll be able to talk with multiple contacts at the same time.

When you're participating in one chat and you receive an invitation to participate in another chat, you can choose the Chat List icon. Each new chat displays the Responding icon. Select the new chat you want to participate in and that chat window will display. On the Blackberry client the Chat List displays as a number of chats at the top of your contact list. Using the Chat List icon, you can move between chat windows, toggle between any of the chats included in the list, or choose to close all chat windows.

Quick responses

You have the option to create prepared responses, also known as "quick responses", which you can store in your mobile device. These are handy when you're on a call or in a meeting, and can't respond to a chat. On a Windows Mobile device, this feature looks like the one shown in the following screenshot:

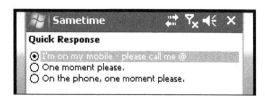

To end a chat, you can select the menu option to **"End Chat"** or **"Close Chat"**. Again, this depends on your mobile operating system as to how this will be displayed, but the function remains the same.

Adjusting Sametime Mobile client preferences

As we discussed in previous chapters, one of the strengths of Sametime is its wide variety of client preferences. The Sametime Mobile client includes a number of the same preferences with which you're already familiar.

For Blackberry users, preferences can be configured under the **Options** menu. Since your screen size is limited on most Blackberry devices, you may want to change the setting for how "offline" people display in your contact list or how messages are displayed in your conversations. Additionally, you can decide if you want to save your message history or show pictures. You can see some of the Blackberry options in the following screenshot:

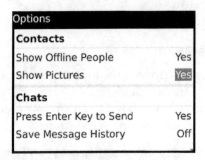

Changing display preferences

For Sametime on Windows Mobile, the **Display Preferences** screen gives you the ability to alter what you see when using the Sametime Mobile client. The focus on the options here is mainly on controlling what displays given the limited screen "real estate" that's available. You are in control when it comes to balancing the size of the information on the screen versus how much information you want to be displayed on the screen at one time.

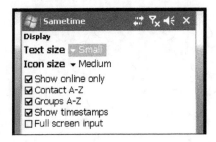

Setting notification preferences

More so than with Sametime running on your computer, it's important to control how the Sametime Mobile client notifies you of incoming information. If you're in an important meeting, you definitely don't want your mobile device making noise every time someone tries to chat with you. You can control whether your device will play a sound, vibrate, or do both whenever someone starts a chat, responds to a chat, or becomes available based on a user alert you set.

You can also control how your mobile device reacts when a new chat or a chat response is received. By selecting the option to bring the chat to the forefront, you can be working in some other mobile application and Sametime Mobile will switch focus back to the chat screen. This can be very useful since you won't have to keep switching back and forth to see if new chat messages have arrived.

Setting up customized status messages

Presence awareness is an important part of Sametime Mobile just as it is in all the other versions of Sametime. The basic four statuses are available to you: **Available**, **Away**, **Do Not Disturb**, and **In A Meeting**:

As with other Sametime clients, you can also customize the status message that others see for your presence awareness. In the following example, users will see that you are available and that you are using your Blackberry as your Sametime client. This could be very useful to people as it lets them know that you are likely away from your computer but you're still available for chatting. Also, when your contacts see your name in their buddy lists, your icon status changes to a mobile device to indicate you're using the Sametime Mobile client. If you don't see a mobile device icon, your Blackberry or Sametime administrator may not have configured this option.

Managing and chatting with Sametime Mobile contacts

Managing your Sametime contacts from your mobile device is similar to managing contacts from your Sametime Connect or Sametime Embedded client. Remember your contact list is available wherever you use Sametime because it's stored centrally on your organization's Sametime server. Any changes you make in any Sametime client will be reflected in any other Sametime client you use.

To add a person to your contact list from Sametime Mobile, select the **Add Person** option.

Start typing the name of the person you'd like to add to your contact list. In this case we started typing "jmehling". Because the name was already in the Blackberry address book, we were able to quickly add it to the contact list. Because your Blackberry is connected to a Sametime server, you can look up names that exist in the Sametime server's directory by typing part of the name, and the same type of lookup will occur on your Blackberry device. We can also choose the group in which to place this contact before we click on **OK** to save this new name in our contact list.

From your contact list, you can select a person's name and then from the menu choose **Person's Info**. You'll see their nickname (if you've created one for them), their system username, their current chat status, and their e-mail address if it is available as a detail in your contact list. The nickname is editable from this view as shown in this Blackberry client:

One nice feature of the Sametime Mobile client on a Windows Mobile device is that it also includes the option to add an "external" person to your contact list. If your organization is using the Sametime Gateway to connect to internet instant messaging services like AOL, Yahoo, and Gmail, you can add that person to your contact list. Select **External User**, and then from the drop-down list select which instant messaging provider they use along with their e-mail address. From this same window you can also select the group name in which to place this new contact.

Blackberry users can communicate with external users who have already been added to their contact list by the Sametime Connect client or the Sametime Embedded client.

Managing your groups from Sametime Mobile

You can add personal or public groups to your Sametime contact list from the Sametime Mobile client.

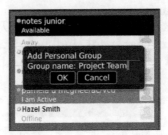

If you'd like to reorganize your groups or rename them from the mobile client, you can! You can select **Rename Group** and change the name of the group. This name change will also be reflected in the group names when you open up your Sametime Contact list from any other Sametime client.

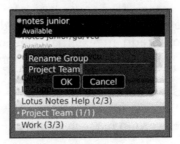

If you want to reorganize your contacts, you can move a contact into a new group with the **Move User** option (Blackberry client).

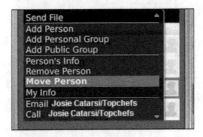

If you have a large contact list with many groups, you may want to consider the **Disable Group** option. This allows you to disable the group rather than delete it so that it won't be included in your contact list. If you're using a wireless internet connection, you sometimes find that network speeds can be quite slow. You can maximize your throughput by only accessing those groups you know you'll need for a particular session. This option is featured in the Windows Mobile Sametime client.

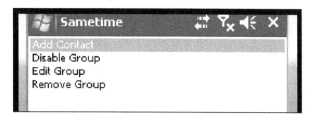

Chat history preferences

Chat history is also something that you can fine tune from your mobile device. Chat history refers to the number of saved messages that will be retained for you. This may be important if you are switching between multiple chats or have to take a phone call and want to see the entire thread of a message. We've displayed the option as shown in the Windows Mobile Sametime client.

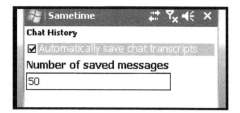

Securing Sametime Mobile

As many of us are painfully aware, mobile devices can easily be stolen or lost. Because of this fact, it's very important to take extra care when protecting the data stored in your mobile device. Information in your Sametime Mobile application is no exception. You want to be sure that your chat conversations are encrypted and that your Sametime password is secured as well.

How is that done? There are several options available for securely connecting mobile devices to your organization's Sametime server:

- Connect with a Virtual Private Network or VPN. A VPN uses a public network like the internet in conjunction with the VPN client to provide a secure tunnel to your organization's network. To provide a VPN connection, your organization may have software available for your device. One such example is IBM Lotus Mobile Connect. Your device first connects to a Mobile Connect server which then acts as an encrypted conduit for your mobile conversations.

- Another method used for Blackberry devices is connecting through the Blackberry Enterprise Server Mobile Data Services, or MDS. MDS acts as an intermediary between your Blackberry device and the Sametime server. It provides a secured connection to your Blackberry device.

- Your organization may have configured an authentication proxy server or an HTTP proxy server. Proxy servers are configured to prevent unauthorized users from obtaining information about the servers connected to the proxy servers. In other words, they act as a shield so that the Sametime server never appears to be connected directly to the Internet.

Your company may have a security policy for mobile devices—check with your system administrator for further information and assistance if you're not sure how to secure your device. While all this may sound very technical and confusing, it's vitally important to the security and privacy of your information, as well as the information of your organization.

Getting help with Sametime Mobile

Just as with other Sametime clients, there is help information available from within the Sametime Mobile client. Click on **Help** and you'll see a menu similar to the following screenshot (our example is from the Blackberry Sametime Mobile client). Different topics are available for context related help.

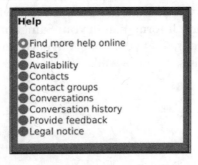

Summary

In this chapter, you learned how to install and configure Sametime on your mobile device. You learned how Sametime Mobile downloads to your handheld device as well as how to login and start a chat session. You learned how to add contacts, set preferences, and how to access your contacts and groups that you have already created via your Sametime Connect or Sametime Embedded client. You learned how to start a chat and use emoticons during the chat session. Finally, you learned the basics of Sametime Mobile security and how to launch Sametime Help files in the Sametime Mobile client.

9
Meeting Basics—Using Sametime to Create Virtual Meeting Spaces

So far you've learned a lot about what you can do with Sametime when it comes to instant messaging as well as voice and video messaging. You've also learned how you can be in touch with your contacts using Sametime Mobile on your mobile devices. In this chapter, we're going to introduce you to Sametime Meeting Center and Sametime Meetings. Sametime Meeting Center is another component of the Sametime software suite that provides a website for online meetings.

Online meetings, also known as web conferences, allow you to collaborate with your colleagues from a web page as if you were sitting in a large conference room face to face, especially as the native Sametime audio and video functions extend to Meeting Center. During a Sametime meeting you can present slides and files and share your screen with the other online attendees. You can even use a virtual whiteboard to brainstorm ideas. Add in the ability to have group and private chats, ask questions, and post user polls, and you have a robust and full-featured environment for holding virtual meetings that bring together your colleagues regardless of where they are physically present. In today's business or organization environment colleagues are not always in the same physical location. More likely they are in different buildings, campuses, cities, states, and countries. Sametime Meeting Center allows colleagues to work together without having to spend time or money for travel.

Working together at less cost—sounds like a winner! Some scenarios for how Sametime Meeting Center could be used include:

- Felicia is responsible for training users on the new financial reporting system and her company has twelve locations in three countries. She can use Sametime Meeting Center to conduct and record a training class and then new users can watch the recorded session, saving Felicia from having to present the class numerous times.

- Camille has a presentation that she wants to share with her team members. She can use Sametime Meeting Center to conduct a virtual meeting, sharing her screen as she displays the slides.

- Libby is using Sametime Meeting Center to present information on a new project that needs a go/no go decision at the conclusion of the meeting. She can use the User Poll feature to allow everyone the opportunity to vote on the final decision.

In this chapter, you'll learn how to:

- Participate in a Sametime meeting and what is required to do so
- Launch Sametime Meeting Center
- Sign into Sametime Meeting Center
- Schedule a meeting
- Save a meeting for later playback
- Create a breakout meeting from the original meeting
- Add slides and files to a meeting
- Send web pages to meeting participants
- Create polls for meeting participants
- Have group chats within a meeting
- Shut down a meeting

What is Sametime Meeting Center?

Sametime Meeting Center is a web-based application where all the Sametime meetings are scheduled and held. Meeting Center is a service of the Sametime server that runs in your organization or company and in most cases is configured to use the same authentication method you currently use to log into Sametime Instant Messaging.

Your Sametime administrator will provide you with a URL of Sametime Meeting Center. It may look something like this: `http://mysametimeserver.com/stcenter.nsf`. When you first enter Meeting Center you can view the list of all meetings, attend an ongoing meeting, schedule your own meeting, or start a meeting instantly from the Meeting Center.

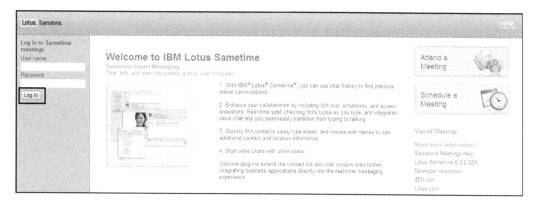

Browser requirements for Sametime meetings

Sametime Meeting Center is accessed using an internet browser. Because the Meeting Center is accessible through the web, you don't need the Sametime Connect client installed in order to use it. Keep in mind that because you are using a web-based application, there are requirements in terms of what browser, operating system, and Java Runtime Environment (JRE) you need to use. The JRE is the "engine" that runs the parts of the Meeting Center that are written in the Java programming language. If you are using Meeting Center for the first time, it may take a few minutes to load up the JRE. It's a good idea to give yourself enough time before the meeting to make sure you can load the software and get logged in with no problems.

Review the following list for the minimum version of software you'll need in order to access Sametime Meeting Center. If you have more updated software, such as Windows Vista, Windows 7, or something similar, you should be able to participate in an online meeting with no issues. If you have questions about what version(s) you might be running, check with your system administrators.

- Supported browsers
    - ° Microsoft Internet Explorer 6.0 or 7.0 on Windows XP Professional, with JRE 1.4.2 or 1.5
    - ° Mozilla 1.7.12 on Windows XP Professional (with Service Pack 2), with JRE 1.4.2 or 1.5
    - ° Firefox 2.0 on Windows XP Professional (with Service Pack 2) with JRE 1.4.2
    - ° Mozilla 1.7.12 on Red Hat Enterprise Linux 4.0 and Novell Linux Desktop 9.0, with Sun JRE 1.4.2 or later
    - ° Firefox 2.0 on Red Hat Enterprise Linux 4.0 and Novell Linux Desktop 9.0, with Sun JRE 1.4.2 or later
    - ° Safari 3.0 on Macintosh OS 10.4.x

- Browser JDK/JRE
    - ° STLinks

The most up-to-date list of requirements can be found on the IBM Lotus site at `http://www-01.ibm.com/support/docview.wss?rs=477&uid=swg27010738`.

Sametime Meeting Center includes a link that allows you to test your browser settings to see if you're ready to participate in an online meeting. Be sure to turn off pop-up blockers in your browser as some meeting functions require pop-ups.

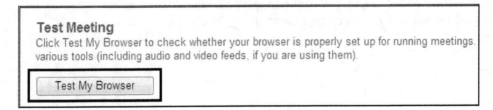

Getting started in Sametime Meeting Center

How do you start a meeting? You can start a meeting from the Sametime Instant Messaging client or from Sametime Meeting Center itself. Meetings are generally scheduled, but can also be created on the spur of the moment. So how do you login and get started? First let's look at security and authentication for online meetings.

Security and authentication for Sametime meetings

As we said earlier, Sametime Meeting Center is a component of your company or organization's Sametime server. Meeting Center provides a secure, encrypted environment for sharing information. Your Sametime Administrator will have customized the configuration of Meeting Center, so you may or may not be required to have a user ID on the Sametime server and login to Meeting Center in order to schedule and participate in a meeting.

However, Meeting Center can also be configured to allow "anonymous" users. If that is the case, you'll be listed as Anonymous for your Meeting Center username when you first connect to Meeting Center. You may be prevented from attending particular meetings if they are restricted to specific attendees but generally you can use Meeting Center much like any other user would, even though you are not signed in.

If you do not sign into Meeting Center before attending a meeting, you'll see an extra dialog box when you enter the meeting. You'll be asked to indicate how your name should show up in the Participant list.

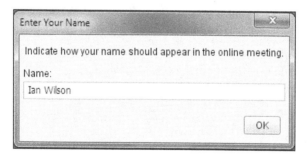

When you are listed in the meeting participant list, you'll see the particular name that you typed in, followed by **/Guest**.

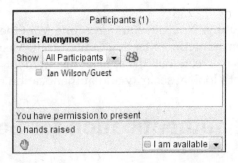

While this is a quick and easy way to get into meetings without taking the time to sign in, it's not recommended if you want to ensure that people know for sure that you were the specific person attending the meeting. An anonymous user can use any name when they attend a meeting, and someone not aware of what **/Guest** means may mistake that person for the actual authenticated user of the same name. For your own protection and to lessen confusion, it is a good idea to always sign in to a Sametime meeting so that your name automatically shows as your authenticated user name. However, if you are using Sametime to let people connect to meetings who do not have accounts on your system this may not be possible. Be sure to educate your users on what **/Guest** means.

Creating a new online meeting

So now with your login information navigate your web browser to the main webpage of Sametime Meeting Center. Once there you'll see two links on the right side of the page to **Attend A Meeting** or **Schedule A Meeting**. On the left side of the page a link to sign in to Meeting Center will be displayed.

One method for creating a meeting is to schedule it in advance. After you log into Meeting Center, you'll see a link in the left-side navigation labeled **New Meeting**. Clicking this link will start the meeting scheduling dialog.

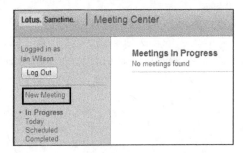

The **New Meeting** panel is used to schedule, configure, and invite attendees to your meeting. The **Essentials** tab of the dialog box has the basic information for the meeting such as the title, description, date, time, duration, and the password. A password is not required for a meeting but you can use that field if you want to make sure that no one enters your meeting without the proper permissions. We recommend you do this as you wouldn't want to have anyone interrupt your meeting who is not meant to be an attendee.

When you set up a time and duration for your meeting, consider your attendees and their schedules. Are they in a different time zone? Is it possible that the meeting may run longer because the topic may require a good deal of attendee participation? Do you want to make this a regularly scheduled meeting? Meetings run concurrently on Sametime Meeting Center. Just like a physical conference room, you can see a listing of the meetings scheduled for a particular day and time.

You can also indicate whether audio or video will be used with the meeting. It's quite common for attendees to use a conventional phone line for voice interaction while using the screen sharing portion of Meeting Center for the rest of the meeting. If you have the network capabilities along with headsets and webcams, you can interact in the entire meeting through the Meeting Center interface.

The **People** tab allows you to decide who should be able to attend the meeting. You can allow all Meeting Center users to join the meeting, or you can restrict it to particular people. If you choose to restrict the meeting, click the **Add or Remove People** button. This will launch a name selection window where you can find and add the people who need to be in the meeting. You're also able to choose whether everyone has the ability to share their screen during the meeting, or whether that feature is restricted to the person who sets up the meeting. For example, restricting access to presenting content is useful if you are using the meeting to display a slide presentation and you don't require that type of participation from the other attendees. To do so, first select the **Restrict the meeting to the following users** option and click the **Add or Remove People** button.

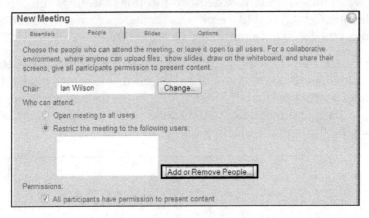

The dialog box that appears lets you choose the people who can attend the meeting. Use the **Search** button to find your attendees and then click on the **Add** button to move them into the **Added Users and Groups** column. When your list is completed, click the **OK** button.

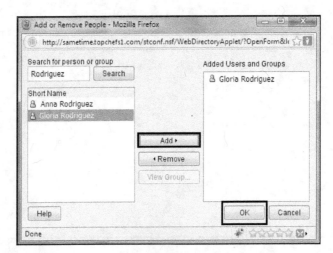

The **Slides** tab allows you to attach a slide file in advance so that it can be viewed during the online meeting. If you choose to add slides, click the **Add Slides...** button, which will launch a window allowing you to choose and upload your file.

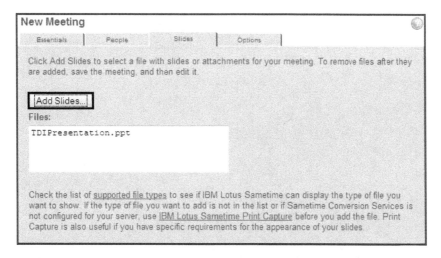

Click the **Browse** button to launch the file selection dialog box that is specific to the operating system you're using with Meeting Center. Once you have your file selected, click **OK** in order to add the file to your meeting.

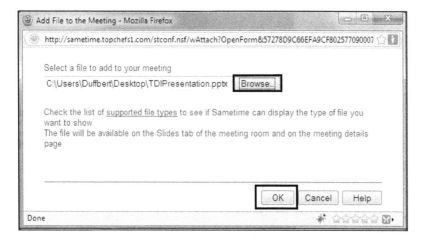

The **Options** tab finalizes the meeting preparation with three additional options. Allowing group chats is the default setting and is a good feature to have in a meeting. People can more easily interact with each other when a group chat is allowed within the actual presentation. The recording option will store the meeting so that others can replay it later. Consider this option if you're presenting a training session, the content of which others will need to view later, and that you don't want to have to repeatedly present to everyone. Be mindful of the fact that stored meetings require significant disk space on the Sametime server so only use this when necessary. Finally, you can make sure the meeting link does not show up in the list of scheduled or active meetings. This is an additional level of privacy that helps to avoid people entering the meeting when they shouldn't be there.

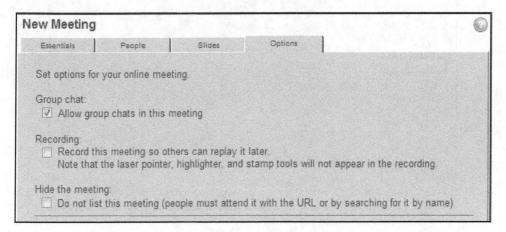

Once all these options are set according to your requirements, click **Save** at the bottom of the page, and your meeting will be scheduled.

Included in the meeting description is a **Link to online meeting**. This is the link that your attendees can explicitly use to go directly to the scheduled meeting. You can include this link in an e-mail with the meeting password information, or the attendees can navigate to your Sametime Meeting Center and check the list of scheduled meetings to determine which one they should attend. Either way, it's easy to provide information to your attendees about the meeting.

Once you've saved the meeting, you go back to the main Meeting Center screen to see your meeting listed as **Scheduled**, **Completed**, or **In Progress**. The attendee clicks on the **Attend** button to join the meeting.

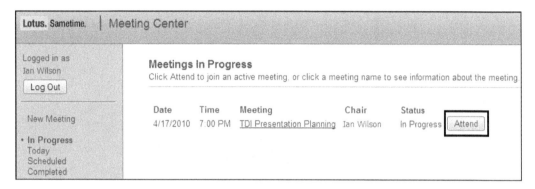

Creating a meeting with the Sametime instant messaging client

You can also create a meeting by quickly using the Sametime Embedded client. From your contact list, right-click on any of your listed contacts, and the **Options** dialog will display a choice called **Instant Meeting**. Once you make this selection you'll see a display to add contacts to the meeting.

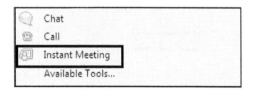

The initial contact you chose will be in the list, but you can also add other names while you are in this panel. You'll notice that the invitee list shows you graphically which contacts have audio or video capability. This is an important consideration if you expect to solicit feedback from the attendees via voice or video during the meeting. However, Meeting Center does incorporate the chat function of Sametime, so they can still participate if they cannot join using headset and webcam.

If your meeting invitee is currently logged into the Sametime client, they will receive a pop-up notification that they have been invited to attend a meeting. They can click **Join** or **Decline** to attend the meeting.

Breakout meeting sessions

While you're in the middle of an online meeting, you may find that you need to pull together a small subgroup of the overall participant list in order to discuss a side issue. Sametime Meeting Center allows you to do this with the use of Breakout Sessions. A breakout session is a completely new and separate online meeting that you can launch from within your existing meeting without having to notify everyone who is in the original meeting.

A breakout session is started by highlighting or selecting one or more names in the Participants List window and then choosing **Actions | New Breakout Session...**.

This action will launch a new window that lists the breakout meeting participants, as well as an area that allows you to invite other people to the breakout meeting.

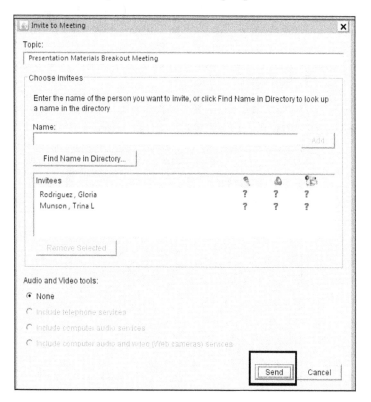

Once you click on **Send**, the new meeting will be created, and people listed as invitees will receive a pop-up invitation to join the new meeting.

There is one element that you need to keep in mind for breakout sessions if you're using audio and video in your meetings. If you start a breakout session, your microphone remains open for both your main and breakout meetings. So if you're discussing sensitive information thinking that you're only being heard in your breakout session, you could be in for an unpleasant surprise.

You should mute your microphone in the main session before using audio in your breakout session. If you do that, then you will only be heard by your breakout session group, and you won't be potentially embarrassed.

Chairing a meeting

Chairing an online meeting is also referred to as being the moderator of the meeting. And just as in a live meeting, the meeting chair of an online meeting is the person who generally starts and stops the meeting and makes sure that the meeting stays on schedule. The moderator has ability to send web pages to the participants, create poll questions, and display the results to the group. They also can assign and revoke privileges for participants, such as the ability to share screens or participate in a whiteboarding session. Generally, the person who creates the meeting is also the meeting chair. The meeting chair is listed in the second tab (**People**) when you are creating a new meeting. It defaults to the name of the person creating the meeting, but it can be changed to be someone else.

If you are unsure as to whom the chair of a meeting is, you can see that information in the **Participants** window of the meeting.

Participating in a meeting

If you receive an invite to an online meeting, you can go directly to Sametime Meeting Center site to find the meeting. Alternatively, the meeting chair might send you a link to the meeting that you can click to go directly there. Either way, you'll see the meeting listed and a button to click for you to attend. When you click the **Attend** button, you'll see a series of messages on your screen as your browser prepares to enter the meeting.

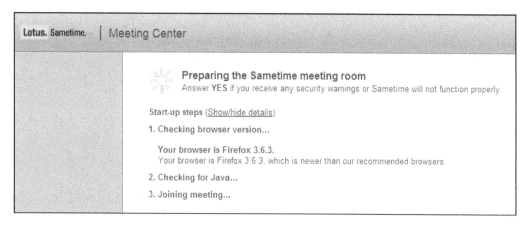

When you first start using Sametime Meeting Center you may be confused by the browser security pop-up windows that may occur when you launch a Sametime meeting for the first time. It's important to answer **Yes** and/or **Run** to any security messages that should happen to appear. The most common message is a pop-up screen that asks if you want to run a Java applet called STLinks. Answer **Run** to this request, or else your meeting will not work properly. You also have the option to always trust the content from this signer. By choosing this option, your browser will always recognize the Sametime applets whenever you launch a meeting, thus eliminating the pop-up windows. As your browser opens the meeting, your entry status will display, and once you've joined the meeting successfully, you will see the Meeting Center environment.

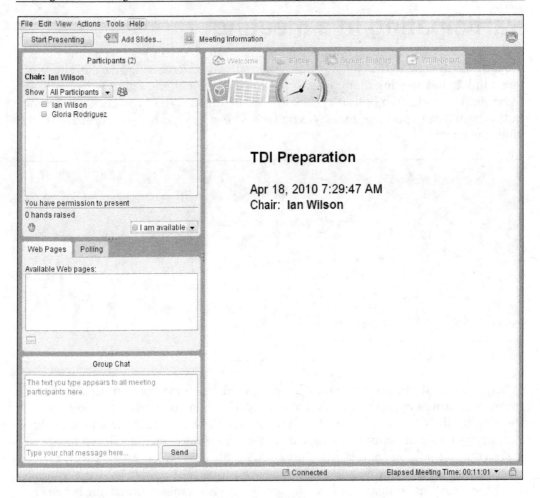

A basic meeting consists of four areas. The **Participant**, **Web Pages/Polling**, and **Group Chat** windows are listed to the left side of the page and are explained in the next section. The **Presentation** area is the large window taking up the majority of the page, and it will be covered in more detail in *Chapter 10*.

The three side windows can be resized based on your preferences for a particular meeting. To resize the window, use your mouse to click and hold the three small dots in between each of the windows. You can then drag the dots up and down to enlarge or reduce the size of the particular window. There are also three dots to the left of the Presentation screen. That allows you to resize the presentation area to have more or less work area depending on what is being presented.

Participant list

Let us now discuss the specific functions of each area. We'll begin with the participant list. It shows everyone who has joined this particular meeting:

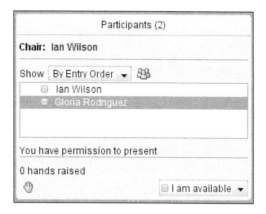

In addition to just showing the participant list, it also gives you a few additional options. You can sort and filter the names using the **Show** drop-down field:

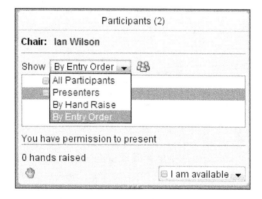

The participant list is also useful if you need to determine who has permission to control the presentation, which participant might have their hand raised to indicate they have a question or a comment, or if you need to know the order in which people signed into the meeting.

You can also right-click on any of the names in order to start a chat with that specific person, or to send them a file that is relevant to the meeting material.

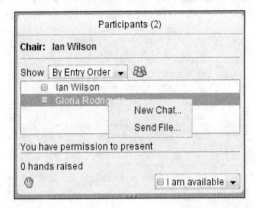

As a participant, you can also change your Sametime availability status from the participant list. Perhaps you need to step away for a minute from the meeting, you can change your status to **I am away** or **Do not disturb** to indicate you're not available.

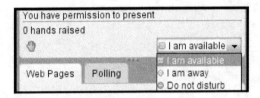

From the Participant list, you as an attendee can also "raise your hand". Use this as an indicator that you'd like to post a question, or present something to the other attendees. When your hand is raised, an indicator will display next to your name, hence the meeting moderator and others in the meeting space can in effect "see" your hand.

Adding web pages to your meeting

The Web Pages feature allows the moderator of the chat to send specific Web URLs to the participants in a chat, and these URLs will open up in a separate browser window. This feature can be useful if during the meeting you need to show examples or pass on additional information. For example, if you were giving a lesson on how to search, you may want to display the Google website for the meeting participants.

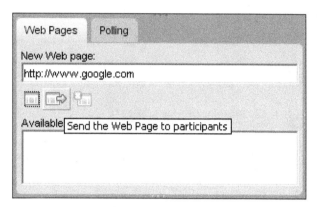

To create a new web page, the moderator enters the URL in the **New Web page** field. By clicking on the middle icon with the green arrow, the web page is sent to the participants. It is also listed in the **Available Web Pages** box for their future reference during the meeting.

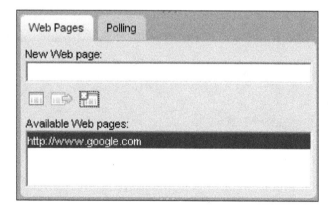

In addition to using the three icons underneath the **New Web page** field, the moderator also has the option to use the menu at the top of Meeting Center to accomplish the same things.

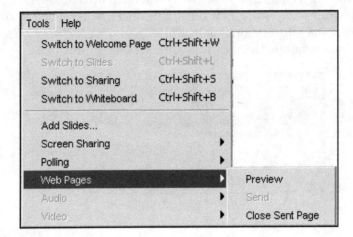

Web Polling

The Web Polling feature is useful for a number of different scenarios within your meeting. The moderator can use a poll to test the audience if the online meeting is being used as a training session. Or perhaps the moderator might use it to finalize a decision in the group by letting everyone vote on whether to proceed in a particular direction.

The Web Polling window appears in the left side of the Meeting Center:

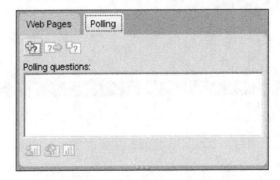

The moderator has the option to add a new polling question by clicking on the question icon with the green plus symbol. A pop-up window appears that allows the moderator to choose the question, the answers, and the formatting. For instance, here is a question format that allows the respondent to choose a single answer from a list:

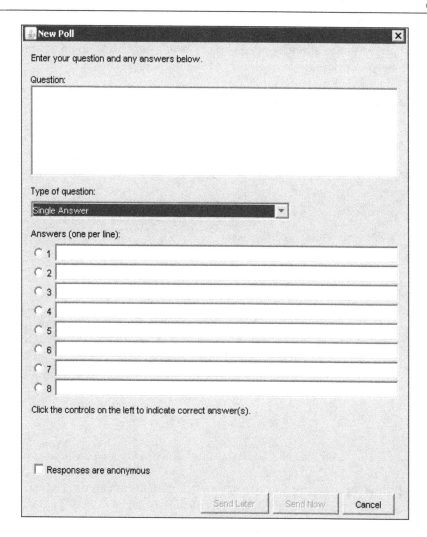

The moderator can also choose whether to allow the responses to remain anonymous or if the responses are tied back to the specific respondents.

The following are the question options that you have available as moderator:

Poll type	Details
Multiple choice – single answer	Up to 8 answer choices are allowed
Multiple choice – multiple answer	Up to 8 answer choices are allowed
Short answer	Text field for answer
True/False	
Yes/No	

The responses are consolidated into a single display screen that the moderator can choose to share with the attendees or keep private. There are also basic statistics and graphing to help with the understanding of the responses.

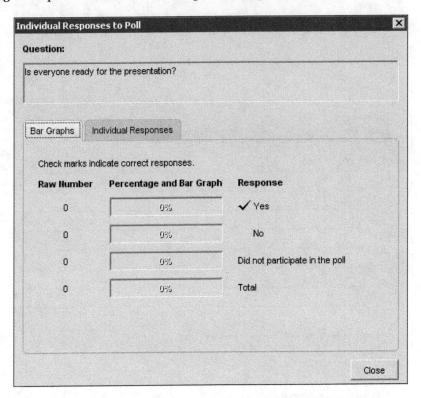

All of the options for creating and displaying the polls also can be controlled from the Meeting Center menu options at the top of the screen.

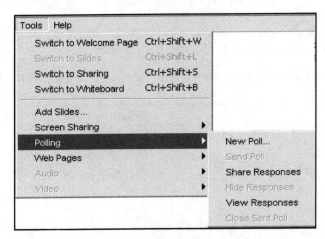

Group chat

The group chat window is a basic Sametime chat designed for all the meeting participants. As this is a "group" chat, anything typed into this window will be seen by all the attendees. So be sure to type only those messages you'd want all attendees to see! Here is an example of how the chat window would look:

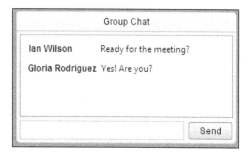

If you want to have a direct chat with someone during the meeting, right-click on their name in the participant window to start a new private chat. This opens a new chat window that only you and the individual person will see.

Leaving or ending a meeting

When you as an attendee are done attending the meeting, you can either just close your browser window or use the menu bar command **File | Leave Meeting**.

This closes your browser window and removes your name from the Participant list.

If the meeting is completely over, it is a good practice to physically end the meeting. To do this, open your browser window that has the Meeting Center site along with the list of active meetings.

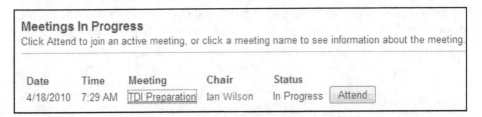

Click on the title to bring up the status page for that meeting. As a moderator you have the ability to end the meeting.

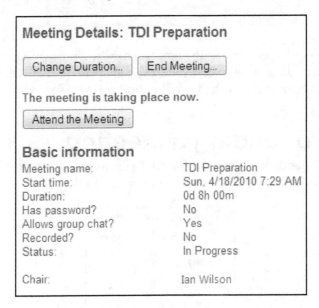

When you click on **End Meeting**, you will be prompted for confirmation, as this action ends the meeting for everyone, even people who might still be in the online meeting space. If you click **OK**, the meeting room shuts down, all remaining attendees are removed from that particular meeting, and the meeting is marked complete.

This is a good practice to follow as it prevents confusion for any attendee who might have arrived late and wonders why no one or only a few participants are in the meeting. It also is important to physically end the meeting if it is being recorded. Otherwise, attendees might join after you have left and enter content that you don't wish to include in the recorded version of the presentation. Ending a meeting also helps to reduce the amount of disk space needed to store the recorded presentation.

Need help?

What happens if you're in a meeting and need some assistance with navigating the meeting? You can always ping the moderator of course. But Sametime Meeting Center does include a help option. Choosing **Help | Help Topics** will display a pop-up window with a wide range of information relating to using the Meeting Center.

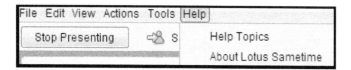

Summary

In this chapter, you've learned how to sign into Sametime Meeting Center. You've learned how to prepare your browser for using Meeting Center. You've learned how to schedule and attend a meeting using Sametime Meeting Center as well as from your Sametime Instant Messaging client. You learned how to configure a meeting so that it will be recorded for later viewing by others. You learned how to create a breakout meeting to discuss side issues during a main meeting. You learned how to add slides and files as the meeting chair. You've learned how to navigate the meeting space as well as how to send web pages and polls to meeting attendees. And finally, you learned how to shut down a Sametime meeting once the meeting has completed.

10
Meeting Beyond the Conference Room—Using Additional Sametime Meeting Features

In the last chapter, we covered the basics of launching an online meeting in Sametime Meeting Center but there are still two major features of online meetings that we'd like to introduce. Meeting Center allows you to share your screen with other meeting attendees as well as allowing you to collaborate on an electronic whiteboard. The whiteboard is especially effective when you upload a file (like a spreadsheet or a Word document) and want to annotate it as a group. Both the screen sharing and whiteboarding features give you the ability to interact with others as if you and the other attendees were in the same room. We'll cover how you can set up and use these features in order to take your use of Meeting Center to the next level.

Some scenarios for how the additional features of Sametime Meeting Center could be used:

- Carl is the technical support person for his department. One of the users has a question about how a certain task works on their computer. Carl can create a screen sharing session in Sametime Meeting Center to display the user's screen and control their cursor to show them how the task works.

- Yun has a spreadsheet that he wants to collaborate on with his team members. He can use the Sametime Meeting Center whiteboard to share the spreadsheet and annotate it to make notes of the changes that need to occur.

- Paul has a new employee working for him in a remote office. Using Sametime Meeting Center, he can set up a virtual meeting with a webcam and microphone to see the new person and talk with them face-to-face.

In this chapter, you'll learn how to:

- Set up a screen sharing session
- Make the most of the Sametime whiteboard feature
- Use voice, video, and audio to accentuate and complement online meetings and conferences
- Save the meeting for future use
- Setup and optimize the audio/video settings built into Sametime Meeting Center
- Learn what steps you can take to optimize network performance during a screen sharing session
- Use best practices and etiquette for online meetings
- Get help if you need it during your meeting

Screen sharing

You've created your online meeting and learned how to invite users and manage participants, and you're ready to begin presenting materials. Let's begin with screen sharing. In order to start sharing your screen in the meeting, you begin by clicking the button labeled **Start Presenting** in the upper-left corner of the window under the menu bar. Clicking that button will enable you to configure your screen sharing session.

After clicking the **Start Sharing** button, the label on the button changes to **Stop Sharing** so that you can hand over control to another meeting attendee if you so desire. The **Start Sharing** button also makes the **Welcome**, **Screen Sharing**, and **Whiteboard** tabs on the main meeting window become active. To start the screen sharing configuration, click the **Screen Sharing** tab.

Clicking the **Screen Sharing** tab reveals yet another row of buttons for you to use to start your session. In this example, you need to click the **Share Screen...** button under the tabs so that you can choose which portion of the screen you'll share.

This dialog box gives you the three choices for what part of your screen will be seen and shared by others:

- **The entire screen**: This makes everything on your computer screen viewable and sharable by others. It is often the easiest and least complicated option as the other attendees will not see blank areas of the screen if you are only sharing a specific application and you change focus on your page.

- **A resizable rectangular frame**: This option allows you to define a certain area of your screen that will be shared, and everything outside of that area will remain private.

- **A currently running application**: This option lists all your currently running windows and lets you share a specific window with other attendees. While this sounds like it's the easiest option, it often causes problems if a dialog box or other message window shows up in your chosen application. It often causes the screen to go gray for your attendees and they won't be able to see what you're doing.

If the presenter chooses the entire screen option, then everything on their screen will be displayed. This includes all the running applications as well as any other applications that may be started during the meeting. Since you have no control over what people might see when something displays on your screen, you may want to make sure to set your presence awareness to Do Not Disturb when using this option. That way no one can send you a message during your meeting that will be seen by all the other attendees.

In the following example, we will choose **A currently running application** to share. We'll select the Microsoft Word document that is currently open on the computer of the person who is sharing their screen.

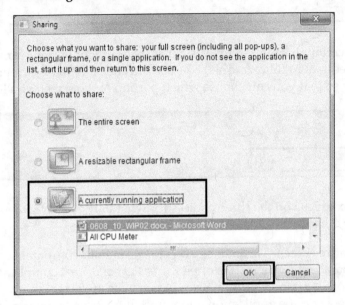

On the computer of the person sharing their screen, an orange box will appear around the application being shared as a visual indication that only that application window is viewable by others. Anything that is done outside that area will not be viewable by others.

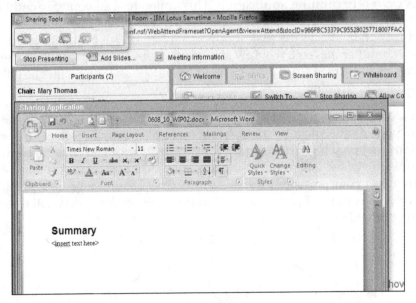

On the screen of the meeting attendee, you'll see that the entire screen sharing session window is taken up by the Microsoft Word application and document. Meeting participants are unable to see anything else on the screen of the person sharing their computer. If the person sharing decides to change the focus of what they are working on during the screen sharing, the window of the other attendees will switch to a gray display.

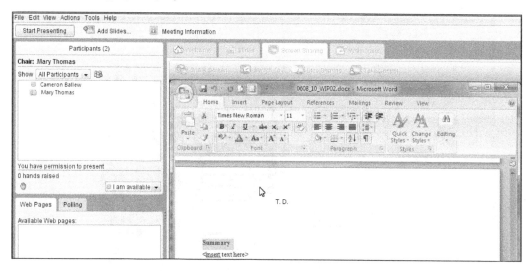

Another option in the dialog box is to share **A resizable rectangle area** of their screen with other attendees. When that option is selected, the presenter can resize an orange-bordered window on their screen, and that portion of the screen is all that the attendees will see when they view the meeting.

This image is an example of what the presenter will see when they select a portion of their screen for viewing.

On the attendee's screen, you can see that they are only able to view a small fragment of the presenter's screen as defined by the orange border. If the presenter resizes the window, the viewable area for the attendees will also resize. Anything that happens outside of that area will not be viewable.

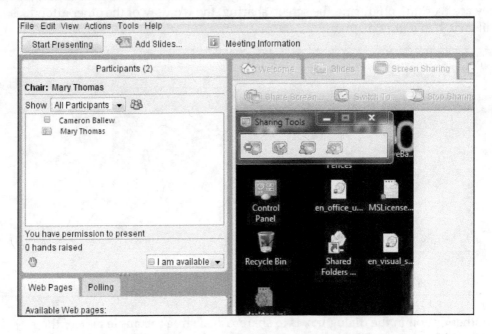

You may have noticed that during a screen sharing session there's a **Sharing Tools** window that can be moved around during the meeting. The icons in that window do the same thing as the buttons under the **Screen Sharing** tab once you start sharing your screen. They also use the same icons so as not to create confusion between the two locations.

- **Switch To...**: This allows you to switch to a different sharing configuration or application. The Sharing dialog box reappears and you can reselect what portion of the screen or what application should be shared.

- **Stop Sharing**: This stops your screen sharing session and lets someone else take over the screen sharing function. Anything that was being shared on your screen is no longer visible to others.

- **Allow Control**: As we'll show shortly, you can display your own screen but let someone else control the cursor and navigation of your computer. The **Allow Control** button gives others the option to do that.

- **Take Control**: This button appears on the screen of the meeting attendees if you clicked the **Allow Control** button. Someone who wants to take control of your screen can do so by clicking that button.

- **Reclaim Control**: This button becomes active if you have given control of your screen to someone else. If you want to stop the attendee from having control of your computer, clicking the **Reclaim Control** button stops the sharing and gives you exclusive control of your computer once again.

As mentioned previously, you can allow someone to control your computer by clicking the **Allow Control** button. In order to see exactly who is moving the cursor on the screen, Sametime adds the initials of the attendee next to the cursor to indicate who is controlling the movements. This is very useful in order to see who is working on the screen at that particular moment so you can talk to the right person during the meeting.

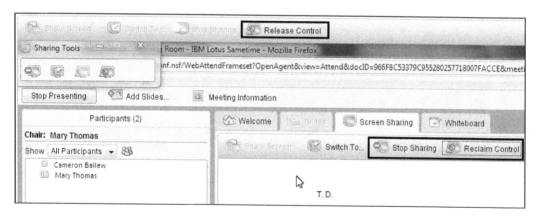

Notice that there are also options to **Release Control**, **Reclaim Control**, and **Stop Sharing**. Each of these allows you to assume some type of control over the sharing session.

There are also two additional icons that you'll find on the far right-hand side of the screen. These two icons control how you view the screen sharing session on your computer.

The icon on the right, a full computer screen, changes your display so that you no longer see the Meeting Center menus and frames. Your entire screen is used to display the displayed area of the presenter. This is useful if the presenter is sharing their entire screen, but their screen size is larger than your viewable area in Meeting Center. Using your entire screen prevents you from having to scroll up and down or side-to-side to view other parts of their screen.

The icon on the left, a computer screen with four inward pointing arrows, returns your full screen display back to the default viewing format of Meeting Center, complete with menus and frames.

Another way to use screen sharing is to use it as a mechanism for assisting other users with issues on their workstations. For example, if you know a team member is having difficulty setting up a macro in a spreadsheet, you could set up a Sametime Meeting with them. By selecting the **Let Others Control My Screen** option, they can share their screen with you, and you could take control of their mouse to show them how it can be done. This is a powerful tool for technical staff as well as for help desk staff.

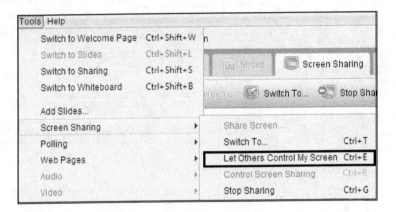

Because this is a powerful tool, you want to be sure you've set a password on the meeting when you created it. You also want to be sure that you're not displaying any inappropriate applications or information on your screen when you share your workstation with others. Finally, end your meeting when you have completed it, so that someone can't access a shared screen if it wasn't closed properly.

Whiteboarding

Whiteboarding is a useful feature when you have a document of some type that needs to be reviewed by a number of people in a meeting, which needs to be annotated for additional information and work. The whiteboard feature can help you do this in Meeting Center by simply loading up a file and starting to diagram your work.

To start a whiteboard session with a particular file, you either need to add the file from the menu or use the file that was loaded by the meeting moderator when the meeting was set up. To add the file(s) from within the meeting, click on the **Add Slides** button at the top of the Meeting Center window.

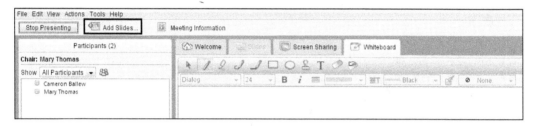

Clicking the **Add Slides** button launches a dialog box that gives you the opportunity to upload a file to the whiteboard area. Click **Browse** and navigate to the file that you want to share on your computer. A copy of this file will be uploaded to the whiteboard area.

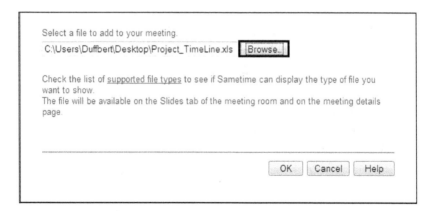

Not all file types are supported in Sametime for whiteboarding. We've included a list of supported file types in Sametime 8.0 for Meeting Center:

File Types	Extensions
Adobe Acrobat, Versions 2.1, 3.0 - 7.0	PDF
AMI and AMI Professional, Versions through 3.1	SAM
Bitmap	BMP
TIFF CCITT Group 3 & 4, Versions through 6	TIF
CompuServe Graphics Interchange Format	GIF
Computer Graphics Metafile	CGM
Hypertext Markup Language (HTML)	HTM, HTML
JPEG file	JPEG, JPG, JPE
Lotus 1-2-3 3.0, 4.0, 5.0, 6.x, R9	WK*, 123
Lotus 1-2-3 97 and 98, R9	123
Lotus 1-2-3 for Macintosh	
Lotus Freelance Graphics for Windows, Versions through 9.6	PRE, PRZ
Lotus PIC	PIC
Lotus WordPro 96/97, R9, text only	LWP
Microsoft Excel for Windows, Versions 2.2 through 2003	XLS
Microsoft PowerPoint for Windows, Versions 3.0 through 2003	PPT
Microsoft Word for Macintosh, 3.0, 4.0, 98, 2001	
Microsoft Word for Windows, Versions through 2003	DOC
OpenOffice Impress, Versions 1.1, 2.0 (text only)	SDD, SXI
OpenOffice Writer, Versions 1.1, 2.0 (text-only)	SXW
OpenOffice Calc, Versions 1.1, 2.0 (text-only)	SDC, SXC
Paintbrush/DCX (multi-page PCX)	PCX
PICT and PICT2 Bitmap Graphics	PCT
Portable Network Graphics	PNG
Revisable Form Text	RFT
Rich Text Format	RTF
Sametime Print Capture File	FST
Sametime Whiteboard	SWB
StarOffice Calc, Versions 5.2, 6.x, 7.x and 8.0 (text only)	ODS
StarOffice Impress, 5.2, 6.x, 7.x and 8.0 (text only)	ODP
StarOffice Writer, Versions 5.2, 6.x, 7.x, and 8.0 (text only)	ODT

File Types	Extensions
Tagged Image File Format	TIFF, TIF, EPS
Text file	TXT, BAT, INI
Windows Metafile Graphic	WMF
WordPerfect for Windows, Versions through 12.0	WPD
WordPerfect for Macintosh, Versions 1.02 through 3.0	
WordPerfect Graphics, Versions 2.0, 7, and 10	WPG, WPG2

Once the file(s) has been uploaded, the icon bar of the whiteboard displays the name of the file and the page numbering. This enables you to switch files during the whiteboard session as well as go to specific pages of each file.

In the following example, we are showing a Microsoft Excel spreadsheet in the whiteboard.

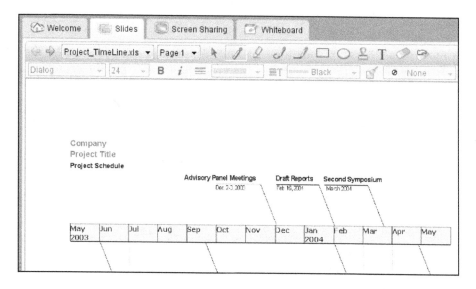

Depending on the size of your screen and the area of the document you need to view, you have a few options in the menu for how to display the whiteboard. You can choose to have the document "fit to screen", which means it will be shrunk or enlarged to fill the available space you have. In most cases, the document will be shrunk down, and some parts may be very hard to view due to the reduced size. You can also choose to display the document in the original size, which means you may only see part of the page on your screen, and you will need to scroll in order to see everything. Finally, you can maximize the document, which means it will take over your entire screen, including the Meeting Center frames and menus.

In our example, we have the spreadsheet set to the original size for ease of viewing.

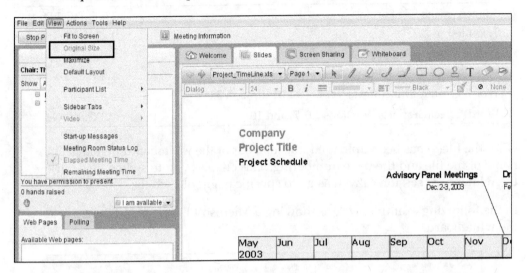

In the following screenshot, we added a number of annotations using the different icon tools. These tools allow you to draw freeform lines, straight lines, rectangles, and ovals. You can also add text, highlight areas of the page, and add star images next to important items. The toolbar under the icons allow you to select different line colors, text sizes, and other tool-appropriate settings. They become active based on which icon you are using at any given time.

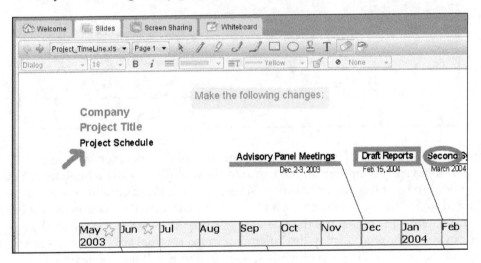

This table explains what each of the items on the icon bar does for you:

Menu item	Meaning
	Advances the file pages forward and backwards.
Project_TimeLine.xls ▾ Page 1 ▾	Allows you to select a particular file that's been loaded into the meeting, as well as selecting the particular page you want to display.
	Change the icon to allow you to select various areas on the screen.
	A "laser pointer" that shows a red dot on the screen that you can use to draw attention to a particular area.
	Highlights a portion of the screen.
	Allows for freeform drawing on the whiteboard.
	Allows a straight line to be drawn on the whiteboard.
	Draws a rectangle on the whiteboard.
	Draws an oval on the whiteboard.
	Places a star image on the whiteboard based on where you click the cursor.
T	Brings up a textbox and places the text at the starting point of the cursor.
	Erases the selected item on the whiteboard.
	Erases everything on the whiteboard.

When you're done annotating, you'll definitely want to save the new version of the file so that you can refer to it after the meeting is over. Meeting Center saves the annotated file in a proprietary `.swb` (Sametime Whiteboard) format that can be used within Sametime, as well as the more common `.rtf` (Rich Text Format) that can be read by most word processing software.

To save the file, use the menu command **File | Save Annotations**.

That starts the process where the files are saved within Sametime. The length of time it takes for the save process is dependent on the size of the files.

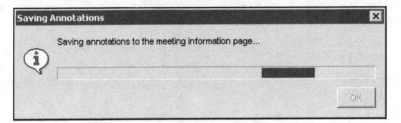

Once the processing is done, you will see the message telling you the file has been saved. Click **OK** to complete the process.

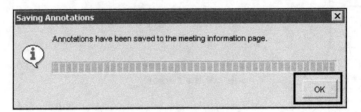

To find the files so that you can download them to your computer, use the menu command **File | Show Meeting** Information.

The dialog box that shows all the meeting information appears on your screen. At the bottom, you will find all the files that were saved as part of this meeting.

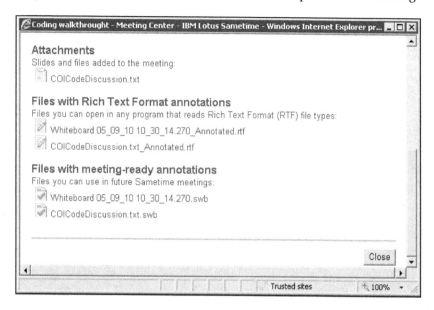

You can save these files by right-clicking on the file names and using the regular file saving routines on your operating system.

Communicating with voice, video, and audio

In a typical organization, it might be very common to use Meeting Center to show your screen or show slides during a presentation while using the phone to talk with all the attendees. Some companies or organizations have a central phone system for conference calls and individuals have the ability to set up conference calls and set up invitations with a PIN number. If you know the majority of your meeting participants don't have headsets or you don't plan to use video during the meeting, setting up a conference call in conjunction with a Sametime Meeting works great and can still save money by eliminating the need for individuals to travel to one central location.

However, Sametime does have an audio and video component in Meeting Center which lets you do it all from within the same software package. If all attendees can connect through a PC or Mac headset and webcam, using the audio and video services of Sametime can also help save money by eliminating the need for long-distance phone charges.

When setting up a meeting, you can activate the audio and video component by making the necessary selection on the **Essentials** tab of the meeting setup dialog box. You can select the **Computer audio** option if you simply want to be able to talk with attendees during the meeting. If you need to be able to see them in addition to talking with them, then choose the **Computer audio and video** option.

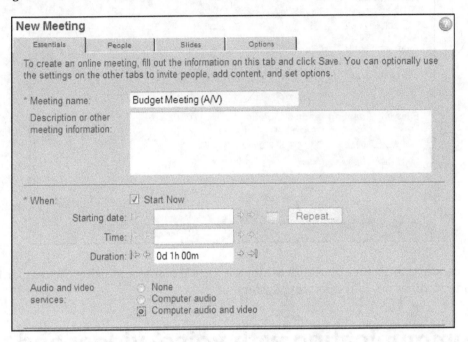

If you select the video option, you'll see an additional tab in the Participants frame in the meeting. The **Video** tab will show either your video picture or the video feed of whoever is talking at the time.

At the bottom of the **Video** tab, there are three icons that control the display and placement of your video frame. The first tab that resembles a right-facing triangle allows your video feed to be active. The second icon that looks like two vertical bars will temporarily stop your video feed so that you aren't visible to other participants. The final icon on the right side that resembles two screens detaches and floats your video frame so that you can move it around on your screen or minimize it to free up more screen space for other parts of the screen sharing session.

At the top of both the **Participants** and **Video** tab, there are icons that control the audio and video settings. The first icon that looks like a speaker brings up a dialog box to allow you to set the speaker volume and the microphone volume. The second icon is a microphone with a slashed circle, which will mute your microphone so that you won't be heard in the meeting. The third icon reverses the muting of your microphone and allows you to be heard again. The final icon has a drop-down menu that allows you to do additional preference setting for your audio and video settings.

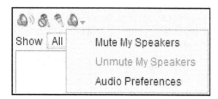

The **Audio** preferences tab gives you the option to pick a particular microphone and speaker set to use on your computer. This might be helpful if you have a microphone on your webcam as well as a microphone attached to a headphone set. You can make sure that the right microphone is being used by the application to pick up your voice.

You are also given the chance to fine-tune your microphone settings so that fewer background noises are picked up during your meeting. This is very useful if you are attending the meeting in some location other than your office, and there is a lot of background noise that you'd like to minimize so as not to distract other attendees.

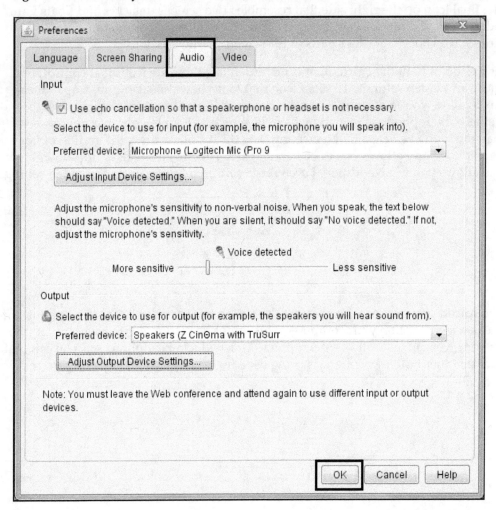

The **Video** tab is similar to the **Audio** tab in that it lets you pick the particular video device you want to use for the meeting. If you have more than one webcam attached to your computer, the drop-down box will list both devices and you can choose between them.

The video source, video format, and size options let you fine-tune the picture quality of your video device based on the type of webcam you are using. You can adjust settings such as color, contrast, and focus. The video format and size option sets the resolution of your video image as well as the compression used to send the video feed. It's important to remember that the larger the resolution, the more network bandwidth that is required and the slower your system will respond. Sametime recommends that you use a 176x144 or 160x120 resolution setting.

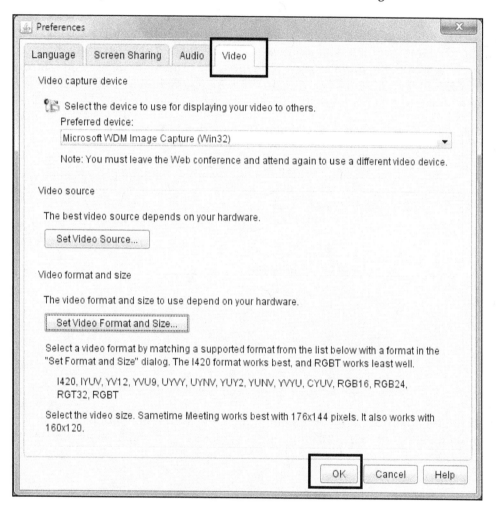

Saving and using meeting materials

As we mentioned, you have the option to record the meeting. This is useful if the meeting can't be attended by multiple participants, is a meeting of record, contains information needed for future meetings, or perhaps you showed a useful slide presentation or training session you'd like to share with other users. Users can login to Sametime Meeting Center and check for recorded meetings.

In the meetings list, you'll see an option for **Recorded Meetings**. If you select this link, a list of recorded meetings will display. Keep a couple of things in mind. First, if the meeting was recorded with a password, you'll need to get the password from the chair of the meeting in order to view it. Second, it's prudent to include a password if you plan on recording the meeting. In this way your content is only accessible to those who know the password.

To replay the meeting, select the **Replay the Meeting** button:

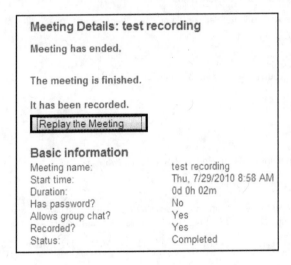

If you are the Chair of the meeting, you'll see a few additional options for the recorded meeting including editing, deleting, exporting, or replacing the meeting.

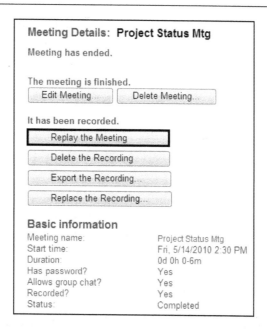

This will open a new browser window for the Sametime Meeting replay. This includes information about the meeting and buttons for you to click to start the meeting replay.

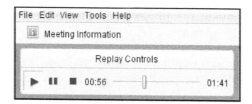

You have the option to use the default layout for the meeting replay, or you can fit the replay to the screen size you are currently using.

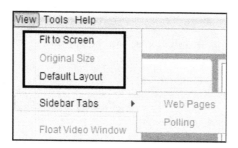

You also have the option to **Play** or **Stop** the recording from the **Tools** pull-down bar.

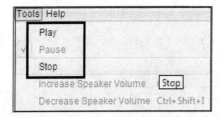

If your meeting included Sametime audio and video those will be included in the meeting recording. You have the option of exporting the meeting recording as it is stored in a .rap file format. This format is proprietary to Sametime. One of the uses of exporting a meeting file is to be able to send it to someone else so they can import it into their Meeting Center and replay the presentation from there.

Best practices for online meetings

When you are working with a screen sharing session, one of the main things to remember is that your network speed, or "bandwidth", will make a big difference in how fast things appear to happen on your screen. While you may not be able to control the amount of bandwidth that you have available, you can control the quality of the images being displayed. The lower you set the quality of the images, the faster the screen will refresh and update.

When you're in a meeting, use the menu command **File | Preferences**. Selecting this option will display the setting for performance in the **Screen Sharing** tab.

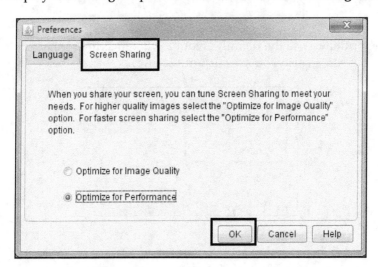

Selecting **Optimize for Performance** will force the system to generate images that are using 8-bit coloring. This means that the colors in the images may not be as clear, sharp, or accurate as the original colors being shown on the screen. Conversely, the screen will be able to update much faster as there is not as much color information traveling over the network lines.

Selecting **Optimize for Image Quality** will retain the image coloring as it is displayed on the computer screen of the presenter (likely 16-bit or 32-bit colors). While the image will be more accurate compared to the original, the speed of the screen might be slower to refresh.

You should use the image quality setting if you are sharing your screen within an internal or local area network that has plenty of bandwidth available. The performance setting is useful if you're conducting a meeting with others who are connecting to the system through internet or wireless access points that may not have adequate download speeds.

Best practices and etiquette for online meetings

Just like the boardroom or breakout room, an online meeting room is a place where you want to put in your best appearance. We're offering a few suggestions to make your online meetings just as effective as if you were meeting in person.

- Send out an agenda in advance, especially if the meeting will be lengthy or have numerous presentations or presenters. This will help to keep the online meeting on schedule and on track.

- As the meeting moderator, send out guidelines for participating when user polls or large number of attendees are to be included. Ask that users raise their hands if they'd like to "speak" online or that they change to mute or to do not disturb mode if they are unavailable for discussion during the conference.

- As a meeting participant, try to attend the meeting on time in order to avoid any confusion or miss any important materials.

- As you're not in the same physical room as the other attendees it may be difficult to determine when a speaker has changed. The meeting moderator or presenter might want to introduce themselves and introduce any speakers as the presenters change.

- When using audio in the room, remember to mute your phone or microphone unless you're speaking. This way background noise or possible office interruptions won't disrupt the meeting.

- Do not mistake the hold button on your phone for the mute button. Often the hold button will cause music to play to the party on hold. Since that's the entire meeting in this case, you are causing a major interruption in the meeting as people will have to talk over the top of your hold music. In many cases, this may cause the meeting to be cancelled and restarted.

- If you are the meeting moderator or presenter, it's a good idea to close any other applications on your workstation so that they don't cause your workstation to crash. Try to avoid working on other desktop applications while you're in the meeting. A crash in an application could cause your workstation to crash and you to drop out of a meeting.

- Advance preparation pays off! If you were making a presentation in a live session, you'd practice, practice, and practice. So don't forget that as a step in your online meeting preparation.

- Try not to send large files to the all the meeting participants. If bandwidth is a consideration, it may be a good idea to send any files to be discussed ahead of time.

- If your speaker includes a poll, be sure to respond in a timely manner. This is especially true if the meeting is on a schedule and your vote is required for a particularly sensitive issue.

- In an online meeting without video, it's important to keep any group chat to the point. Try to minimize any sarcasm or commentary that isn't available to the entire group.

- After the end of meeting, send out a summary of the meeting minutes to all invited attendees.

- Finally, since many organizations record their online meetings, what you say and present is a matter of record and reflects on you professionally and personally. Think before you type.

Need help in the meeting center?

Meeting Center, like all other parts of Sametime, comes complete with Help files that will answer your questions as you're using it. You can select **Help** from the toolbar. Also, in the upper-right corner of most screens, you'll see a blue question mark link that provides context-appropriate help for wherever you are.

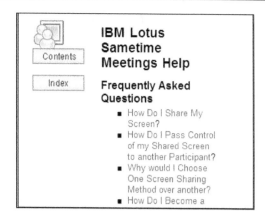

Summary

In this chapter, you learned how to set up a scheduled meeting as well as how to attend a meeting that has already been set up. You learned how to share various parts of your screen during a meeting, be it the entire screen, a single application, or even a small defined area of your screen. You learned about the whiteboard function, and how you can load a file into the whiteboard area for group sharing. Once in the whiteboard for a file, you learned how to annotate the file and how to save those annotations after you are finished with your meeting.

You learned how to use voice and video to enhance your meeting and make information sharing even easier. You learned how to configure your audio and video settings to get the best performance in the meeting based on the type of connection you have. You also learned the types of practices and behaviors that make for productive meetings. Finally, you learned how to access the help files in Meeting Center to get general and context-sensitive help.

11
Take Your Instant Messaging to the Next Level—Sametime Advanced

Sametime Advanced, our topic for this chapter, adds several powerful features to your Sametime experience. The first feature is the Sametime Advanced chat room which is similar to what you may have used with other Instant Messaging tools like Skype or AOL. Additionally you can create and join broadcast communities and utilize a number of tools like polling and announcements.

Some scenarios for how the features of Sametime Advanced could be used include:

- Sophie is heading up a new project team that spans multiple time zones. She wants to have an ongoing chat that everyone can participate in without losing any content. She can set up a persistent chat room in Sametime Advanced that allows her to do this.

- Keela needs to be able to send immediate announcements to all the members of the emergency response teams in her company. She can use Broadcast Community in Sametime Advanced to specify all the members and use the Broadcast Chat feature to send the announcement and start a Broadcast Chat related to the announcement.

- Filip needs to review a proposal document with a member of his Broadcast Community. He can use the Instant Share feature to share his screen with the other person and start the document review.

However, there is something to keep in mind. Sametime Advanced is a separate product from the main Sametime product that we've talked about up to this point. It may be that your Sametime administrators have not chosen to implement Sametime Advanced, so you may not find these features in your environment. If you have any questions on whether Sametime Advanced is available to you, please contact your Sametime administrators.

In this chapter, you'll learn how to:

- Access Sametime Advanced through a web browser
- Start your own chat room or find a chat room that includes a topic in which you're interested
- Manage your chat room users and transcripts
- Utilize Sametime Advanced features using the Sametime Connect and Notes Embedded client for chat rooms and features within the broadcast community
- Access a broadcast community and learn how to create your own
- Use the features of a broadcast community including Skill Tap, Instant Poll, Broadcast Chat, and Announcements
- Use Instant Share with your Sametime Connect client to immediately start sharing your workstation or application with others, without requiring access to a Sametime Meeting Center to do so

Getting started with chat rooms

So what exactly is a Sametime Advanced chat room? Chat rooms let you start discussions with one or more Sametime users on a particular topic. What makes a chat room different from the Sametime chat window is that the chat room conversation is persistent over time. When you're not signed in, the chat room continues to exist and saves the conversations of all members of the chat. When you sign back into the chat room, you can review the activity that occurred while you were offline, and then continue with the conversation just as if you never left. These chat rooms can be either public or private, so you can use them as a company-wide room or restrict it to just a small group of people who are involved in a task. Chat rooms can be created and accessed from a web browser, Notes Embedded client, and the Sametime Connect client.

Using chat rooms in a web browser

Let's begin by accessing chat rooms from your web browser. The Sametime Advanced server that controls the chat room feature uses a slightly different web address than the address of your regular Sametime server. Your Samtime administrators will provide you with the URL address to begin using the Sametime Advanced website. As with Sametime Meeting Center, you'll be required to login to begin using the features. Your login will most likely be the your Sametime user ID, but if you're unsure, check with your Sametime administrator.

When you complete your login process, the Sametime Advanced home page that focuses on the chat room and broadcast community features will be displayed. It looks very different from Sametime Meeting Center, but is very easy to navigate. One of the first things you'll notice are the tabs across the top of the window that indicate what types of features you can access. These include **My Chat Rooms**, **All Chat Rooms**, and **Broadcast Communities**.

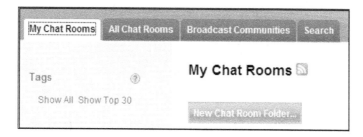

To start a new chat room, click on the **All Chat Rooms** tab at the top of the screen and then click on the **New Chat Room** button.

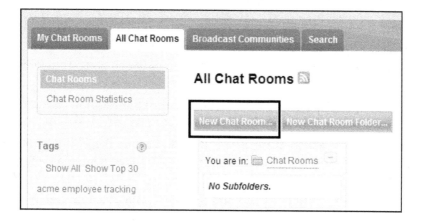

Clicking the **New Chat Room** button opens a dialog box that walks you through the options you have available for a chat room setup.

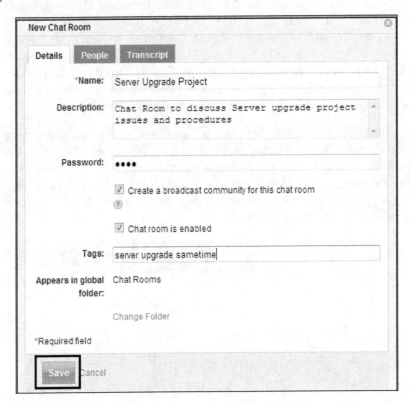

On the **Details** tab, you have the following information:

- **Name**: A required field that identifies the chat room. This will be the name that appears in the lists of all the available chat rooms.

- **Description**: A more complete description of the chat room to help others understand the topic that is being discussed.

- **Password**: You can create a password for the chat room in case the information is sensitive and should only be accessed by specific individuals.

- **Create a broadcast community for this chat room**: Select this option if you also want to create a broadcast community with the same name for this chat topic.

- **Chat room is enabled**: If you want the chat room to be immediately available, select this option.

- **Tags**: Tags are used to assign short words or phrases that categorize the chat room for searching and grouping.

- **Appears in global folder**: You can assign chat rooms to a specific folder for grouping purposes. The default option is the highest level folder called Chat Rooms.

The **People** tab allows you to select the individual or individuals who will manage the chat room as well as identify those members who might be eligible to join:

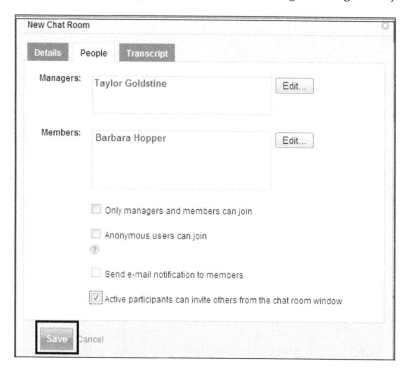

- **Managers**: People who have the ability to administer the chat room
- **Members**: People who are members of the chat room
- **Only managers and members can join**: This restricts the membership of the chat room to those who have been specifically added in the above two fields.
- **Anonymous users can join**: This allows people who are not included as explicit members, but who are in the Sametime directory to participate in the chat. You might use this option for a corporate helpdesk chat or an open forum discussion.
- **Send e-mail notifications to members**: This option will send an e-mail notification to the members of the chat room when the room is created.
- **Active participants can invite others from the chat room window**: If the chat room is not restricted to specific people, this allows chat participants to invite others to join.

If you add people in the **Managers** and **Members** field, you will see a dialog box that allows you to find and add people from the Sametime directory. Once all the people are added, click the **OK** button to add them to the chat room.

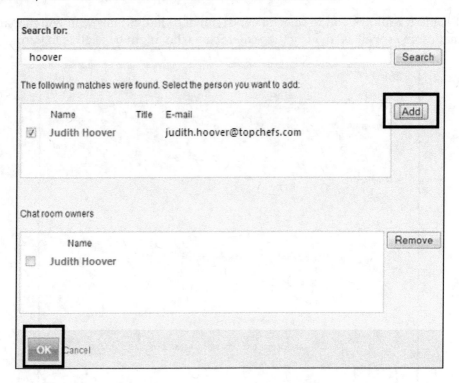

The final tab labeled **Transcripts** controls how much information is shown in the active chat window.

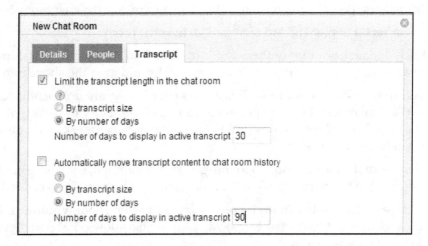

- **Limit the transcript length in the chat room**: Hide the active chat window activity after so many days or number of lines

- **Automatically move transcript content to chat room history**: Move the content from the active chat window to an archive area after so many days or number of lines.

Once all these fields are filled in, click the **Save** button at the bottom of the screen and the chat room will be created.

To enter the chat room, click on its title. This brings up the entrance page for the chat room.

Entering the room provides you with the chat room interface that has the frames for active participants, files, chat transcript, and chat text entry area.

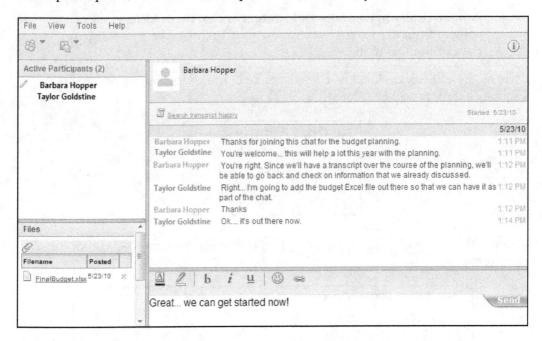

The Chat and **Active Participants** areas are very similar to what you're used to seeing with a regular Sametime chat. To add a new file to the chat room, simply click on the paperclip icon in the **Files** frame and select the file from your computer.

The menu provides additional options and features for working with your chat room.

File | Save Chat Room Transcript gives you a way to save a chat transcript to an HTML file on your computer. **File | Open Chat Room History** brings up a Sametime page that has the transcript of the chat room displayed.

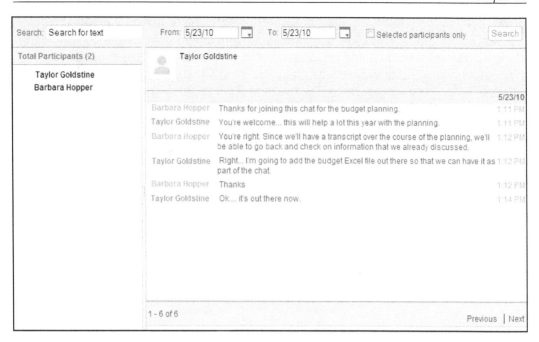

Within the chat transcript, you can search for specific text, narrow the search by dates, and also restrict the search to selected participants.

You can also archive the transcripts of your chat rooms. You may want to do this if a room is particularly active or includes a lot of attachments. It might make sense for you to archive every week or every month depending on how many members and conversations are taking place in the room. To archive the transcript, click the **Manage Chat Rooms** icon. This will open the Sametime Advanced Browser window. Select either **All Chat rooms** or **My Chat Rooms** and select the name of the chat room you wish to archive. In the chat room details, click **More Actions**, then **Archive**. If you do not see this displayed, you may not have access to archive your chat room. Check with your Sametime administrator to verify that you have the appropriate access level.

The **View** menu option customizes what you see in the chat area.

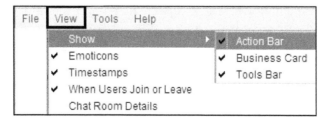

View | Show | Action Bar turns the icons under the menu bar on and off.
View | Show | Business Card turns the name and avatar area for the user above
the chat transcript area on and off. **View | Show | Tools Bar** turns the chat toolbar
(for emoticons, hyperlinks, and text formatting) on and off.

The rest of the **View** options control what is or is not seen in the chat transcript area.
View | Emoticons will turn the display of emoticons in the transcript on and off.
View | Timestamps turns the time displays to the right of the chat lines on and off.
View | When Users Join or Leave will add transcript entries showing when users
join or leave the chat room. Finally, **View | Chat Room Details** displays a new
window that has a summary of the chat room details.

The **Tools** menu option sets your presence awareness status, as well as giving you
the ability to invite others to the chat room, add a new file to the chat room, or to
insert an emoticon or hyperlink into the chat.

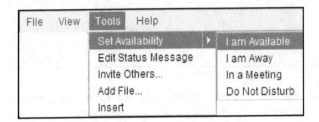

The **Action Bar** in the chat room gives you a couple more capabilities in your chat
room. The **Invite Others** option will give you a dialog box similar to the one you
saw when you selected managers and members for your chat room. These may be
individuals who are already members of the chat room or anonymous users who
are not members (depending on the security settings of the chat room).

The **Chat Room FAQ**, or "Frequently Asked Questions", allows you the option to
create an on-going list of questions and answers for the chat room. FAQs save you
a lot of time because you don't have to repeatedly answer the same questions about
the chat room or the topic. To begin adding a new frequently asked question, click
the **Add Chat Room FAQ** button.

When the **Add Chat Room FAQ** option is selected, a new window appears that allows you to add a new question to the FAQ. The question is limited to 512 characters, and the answer has a limit of 2048 characters.

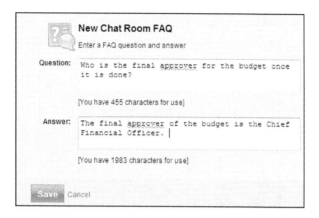

Once you click the **Save** button, the FAQ entry is added to the FAQ for this particular chat room.

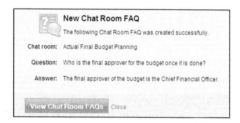

If you want to review the entire FAQ, you can view it by clicking the **View Chat Room FAQs** button in the window or by selecting the Action Bar icon for opening the Chat Room FAQ.

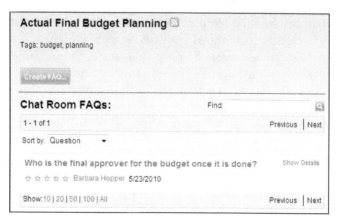

The Chat Room FAQ page lists all the FAQ entries with the title, author, and date of the entry. You can display the answer for a question by clicking on the **Show Details** link next to the questions. The stars next to the author's name also gives you the ability to rate the quality of the question and answer. When you click on the stars, a window appears that allows you to rate the answer.

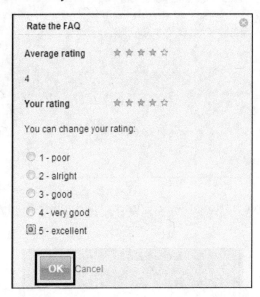

This feature will, over time, show which answers are most popular based on how useful people found the answers.

Using chat rooms in the Sametime Connect client or Notes Embedded client

When you are using chat rooms within the Sametime Connect or Notes Embedded client, most of what you learned from using chat rooms in the browser still applies. In order to access Sametime Advanced features, your Sametime administrator will have provided the Sametime Advanced plug-in as part of your Sametime Connect or Notes client installation package. We briefly touched on installing new plug-ins for the Sametime Connect client in *Chapter 3*. For our next examples, we're going to use the Sametime Connect client, but you'll see many if not all of the same icons and toolbars in the Notes Embedded client. When you are connected to a Sametime Advanced server in your Connect client, you'll see two new panels titled **Broadcast Communities** and **Chat Rooms**. Expand the Chat Rooms panel by clicking on the title bar. Under the chat room bar, you will see that in this example this user is a member or manager of three chat rooms.

To search for more chat rooms, you simply click the magnifying glass icon in order to search for chat rooms by name.

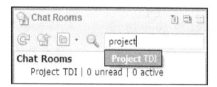

Remember we mentioned earlier that conversations in chat rooms are persistent. Other members of the chat can be using the chat room when you aren't there, and you can go back in at a later time to catch up on the activity. If you want to find out if others are in the chat room or if there are unread messages, you can click the circular arrow icon and it will refresh the details of the chat room in your Connect client. You'll notice that the status may change to show how many members of the chat room are actively logged in and also how many new postings have occurred since you were last in the room.

Next to the circular arrow icon, there is a star icon that, when clicked, allows you to find and manage your chat rooms. This opens the very same web page we used previously to create a chat room from the browser. You'll notice that you didn't have to login to the browser, as Sametime Advanced uses single sign-on to pass your credentials from the Sametime Connect client or the Notes Embedded client to the Sametime Advanced server.

One last icon to note in the Chat Room toolbar is the folder icon. Clicking the folder icon gives you different options on how you want to list your chat rooms in the Connect client.

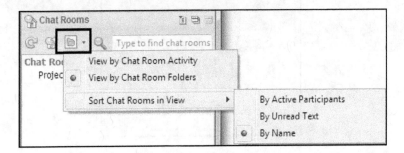

So you now have your list of chat rooms. How do you manage them? From your Connect client, you can right-click the name of the chat room to get a drop-down menu of chat room management options.

Using the **Enter Chat Room** option launches a Sametime Connect chat window very similar to what you'd see with a regular chat window.

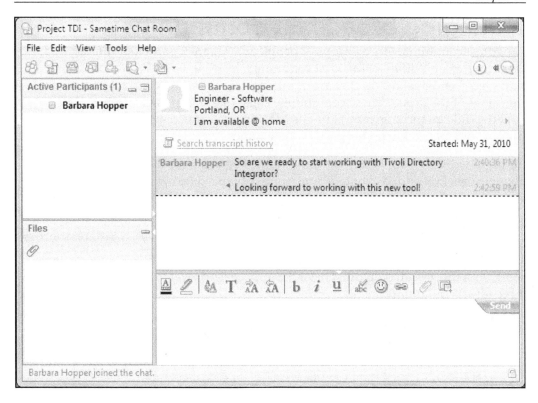

From the discussion of the Chat Room layout earlier in the chapter, all the main portions of the screen should look very familiar. The icons on the action bar are also the same as the icons from the chapter on the Connect client chat, with the addition of two new icons at the end. The next to last icon with the question mark displays the Chat FAQ options, both to add a Chat FAQ entry or to read the entries that are already out in the FAQ area. The last icon in the action bar that resembles two screens with an arrow is to start an Instant Share screen sharing session. The options to share an application, a region of your screen, or your entire screen are identical to what we covered in the chapter on having screen sharing sessions.

On the action bar on the far right side of the chat window, you'll see two additional icons that are unique to chat room usage. The first icon with the lower case "i" will launch a small window with the chat room details, such as the name and description of the room, the level of access, and other details. You can also remove the chat room completely from this screen. The other icon resembling the discussion bubble with left-facing arrows will expand and collapse the chat transcript area.

Managing broadcast communities

Broadcast communities are groups of people who share a particular interest in a topic or project. Within a broadcast community you can have discussions, share news feeds and bookmarks that are of interest to others, and conduct polls and ask questions of the group. These communities, just like chat rooms, can be public or private, and can serve as central points of reference to keep everyone informed and to bring others quickly up to speed on new topics.

To begin working with broadcast communities you can use the Sametime Connect client, Notes Embedded client, or Sametime Advanced browser window. To use all the features of a broadcast community requires the use of the Sametime Connect client or Notes Embedded client. For our examples we will use the Sametime Connect client.

Broadcast Communities appear as another panel in the Sametime Connect client. To work with this feature you must have the appropriate level of access to join or create a broadcast community.

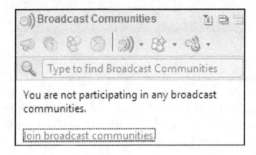

When you create a chat room, an option is included to create a broadcast community at the same time. You can also create a broadcast community by selecting the **Join broadcast communities** link in your **Broadcast Communities** panel. A pop-up window will appear that allows you to either join existing communities or start a new one.

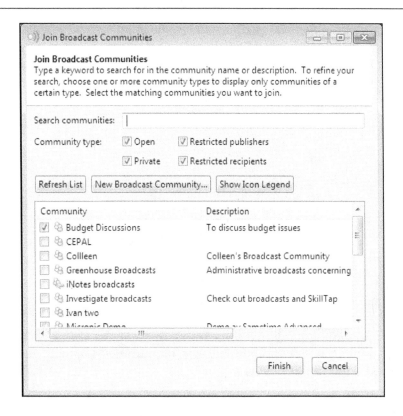

To create a new broadcast community, simply click on the **New Broadcast Community** button. This launches a browser window asking for the basics such as name, type, and descriptions. The **People** tab is similar to the People tab you saw when setting up a new Chat room.

The **Type** field determines how people will be able to interact with the community. It can be **Open, Private, Restricted Publishers,** or **Restricted Recipients**. The small people icons next to the community name signify what type of broadcast community it is. Clicking the **Show Icon Legend** button displays a pop-up window that describes the nuances of each type of community.

Once you have joined one or more Broadcast Communities, they will be listed in your Broadcast Communities panel.

Communities are beneficial in that they allow you to send out group announcements, start broadcast chats, conduct instant polling, and find the experts on a particular topic (using the Skill Tap feature). You can start these four options by clicking on one of the first four icons in the Broadcast Community panel, or you can double-click on the name of the community. This launches a pop-up window that allows you to select which Broadcast application you want to start.

Announcement broadcasts are designed to send a message to each member of the community to alert them to some particular event or piece of information. The Announcement window allows you to type in a message that will be sent to everyone, as well as giving you the option to start a chat associated with that announcement.

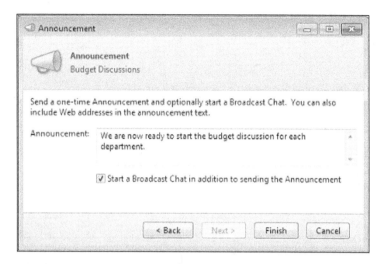

Skill Tap announcements are designed to find answers to questions that members in the community might have. The Skill Tap window has an area for the question, and then a button that searches the Broadcast Community FAQ for potential answers.

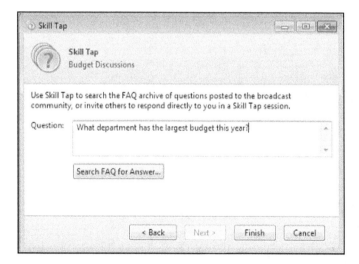

Broadcast Chats allow you to start ad-hoc group chats with everyone who is a member of the community. The members will get a notice of the chat, and can then join in.

Instant Polls are useful for getting instant feedback and voting from the community members on a particular issue. The person starting the Instant Poll enters the question along with the potential answers. If more than one answer is allowed, select the **Allow Multiple Choice Response** option.

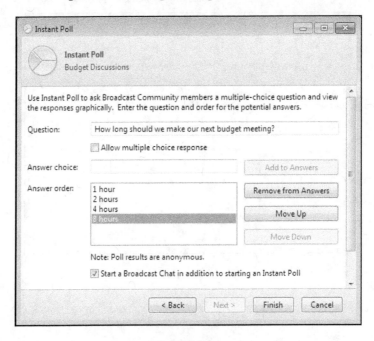

When the **Finish** button is clicked, all members of the community will be notified of the poll through a pop-up window. They can answer the poll as well as see the results to date.

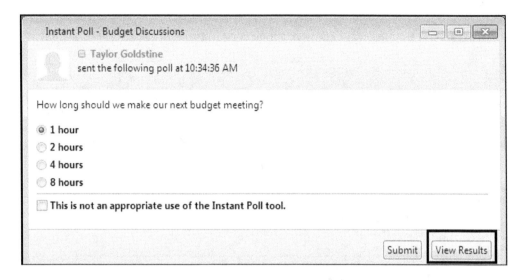

By clicking the **View Results** button, you can see what answers have been received up to that point in time.

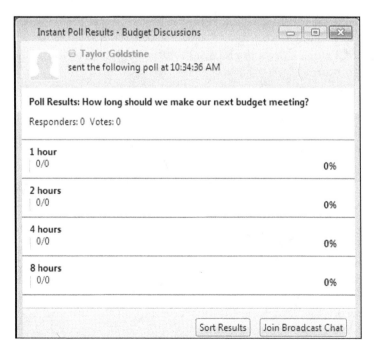

The final three icons on the action bar for the Broadcast Communities panel manage the communities you are part of.

The icon that portrays sound coming from a speaker manages the broadcasts you receive. You can allow or block all broadcasts, or you can work in the **Filter Incoming Broadcast** screen to selectively allow or block certain types of broadcast messages.

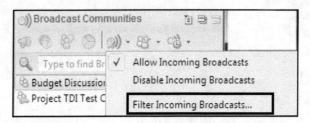

The second icon that looks like two people allows you to join broadcast communities or create new communities for others. You can also edit existing broadcast communities such as updating who has manager privileges.

The final icon of a clock shows the recent broadcasts that you received, as well as the FAQ for the community.

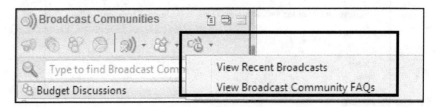

Using instant share

We introduced screen sharing in the last chapter as a feature of Sametime Meeting Center. Sametime Advanced allows you to "instantly" share your screen or an application with one of your Sametime contacts. The Instant Share function is only available from the Sametime Connect client or Notes Embedded client.

To start an Instant Share session, open a chat window or click on the name of one of your Sametime Contacts. Click the Instant Share icon and select the portion of your screen you want to share.

For example, if you're only going to share a region or portion of your screen, you would select that option. A window will display indicating that the screen sharing is initializing, and then you will see an orange bordered area that you can adjust to select the region which you'd like to share with your contacts. You can end sharing or add additional users within the Screen Sharing toolbox that will also be displayed.

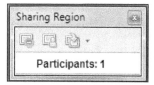

Instant Share works with those who are members of your Sametime community. You cannot share with any individual who has set their status to **Do Not Disturb**.

Sametime geographic locations

When you are working with team members who travel frequently and who may be in different time zones to yourself, it's important to see where your contacts are located when you're setting up chat rooms or broadcasting announcements. One feature included in Sametime Advanced is the tracking of geographic locations. When you click on a contact name, even if the person is offline, the last geographic location will be displayed. If you change to another location where another Sametime user in your community has been, the new location information will be included in your business card display.

Rosa Baldacci
I am Active @ Home Office
Server Community: Sametime (stadv.topchefs.com)
Location: Richmond, Virginia
Time Zone: Eastern Time
Last Chat: 4 days ago

Geographic locations are added by modifying your Sametime preferences. You can select the option to **Share my location information with other users** to make sure that your contacts may see your location.

When you need help

Much like every part of Sametime we've discussed throughout the book, Sametime Advanced comes with Help and About files to help you get answers to your questions. If you click on the **About** link in the upper-right corner of the Sametime Advanced browser window, you see a very helpful page of information that will allow you to dig even deeper into chat and community features.

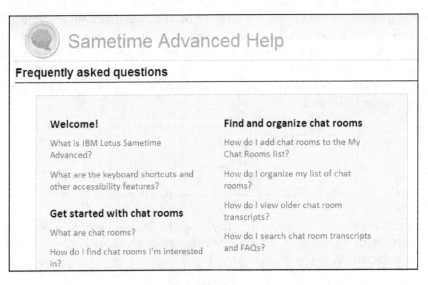

Even if you don't have a specific question, we recommend you to go through the About links just to give yourself a more complete picture of what Sametime Advanced can do for you. The **Help** link in the upper-right corner of the Sametime Advanced browser window will provide you with a more traditional set of links to help file material.

Between these two resources, you should be able to find the answer to just about any question you have.

Summary

In this chapter, you learned about the additional features that Sametime Advanced adds to the Sametime environment and how it can further extend your communication with your colleagues. You learned how to create a chat room and how to invite people to participate in the chat. You learned about the persistence of the chat within the chat room and how that can be useful. You also learned how to manage the chat room transcript so that it is displayed and archived according to your needs. Finally, you learned how to create a chat room FAQ to answer questions, as well as how to vote on FAQ answers according to their quality.

Next, you learned how to create a broadcast community using the Sametime Connect client and the Notes Embedded client. You learned how to create announcements, Skill Tap questions, ad-hoc chats, and instant polls to assist in the decision making process.

Finally, you learned how to start instant screen sharing sessions from within Sametime Advanced. You also saw how Sametime Advanced stores geographic information so you can see where your chat participants are located. Finally, you learned how to access the Sametime Advanced Help files for additional assistance.

12
Speak Up—Taking Advantage of Sametime Unified Telephony

In previous chapters, we've covered an incredible amount of information on how Sametime can help you communicate and collaborate with co-workers and partners. You can exchange instant messages, share your screen, create chat rooms, and have others see you through video. These tools, along with all the other features of Sametime, help you to be more efficient and effective in getting things done.

But there's still one more method of communication that you use every day that we haven't touched on, and that's your telephone. Picking up the telephone to call someone is so common that we often don't even think about it. But is there some way that Sametime can be incorporated into your phone system to make your communication experience even more integrated and complete?

Yes! Sametime offers a telephony integration feature when you install Sametime Unified Telephony (SUT) that ties your telephone system into your Sametime client. Sametime Unified Telephony requires additional hardware and software installed in your organization's server environment that links to your Sametime server. Your organization's network or telecommunications group may also be involved in the implementation of Sametime Unified Telephony as it integrates with your company or organization's phone system. You should ask your Sametime administrators if SUT is installed in your organization.

What does this mean for you as a Sametime user? With SUT you can do such things as see whether someone is on the phone or not, have a single number to reach your colleague wherever they may be, route your calls to different locations based on routing rules, and use your computer to make phone calls over the computer network using a technology called Voice over Internet Protocol (VoIP). VoIP can save you significant amounts of money as it bypasses the normal phone system and uses your internal network or your Internet network connection to make calls.

Some scenarios for how the features of Sametime Unified Telephony could be used include:

- Deepthi needs to place a phone call to another member of the purchasing department. By using SUT, she can place the call on her computer using a headset and microphone without incurring any long distance charges.

- Haru is talking with a member of the Customer Service team to answer a question related to a subscriber benefit. He can use SUT to add Angelina onto the call as she has the information that is needed to resolve the issue quickly.

- Cesaro spends a significant amount of time traveling, and he wants to have all his office calls automatically routed to his cell phone. He can use SUT to set up call routing rules to make sure this happens.

In this chapter, you'll learn how to:

- Place a phone call using SUT

- Answer a phone call sent to your computer

- Add another person onto a currently active call

- Transfer a call to another person

- Save the phone numbers and devices you want to have recognized by SUT

- Set up rules that will route calls based on your Sametime status

What is Sametime Unified Telephony (SUT)?

If your organization is using SUT, you will see a few minor additions on your Sametime Connect or Notes Embedded client (for Windows, Macintosh, or Linux). In addition to the awareness presence icons next to your contact names, you might also see a phone icon to show that your contact is available to receive phone calls using SUT. For example, a blue phone icon shows that your contact is on the phone. The green phone icon in the toolbar is context sensitive. If you have one of your contact names selected, you'll see the option **Call Selected Contact** if they are able to receive a call. If they are not able to receive a call because no phone number is listed for them or they are not using SUT, you won't see that option. If you and your contacts are logged into a Sametime community that uses SUT, when you select the green telephone icon—if you select a contact who is not using SUT, your options will be: **Call a phone number**, **Sametime Phonebook**, or **Call History**.

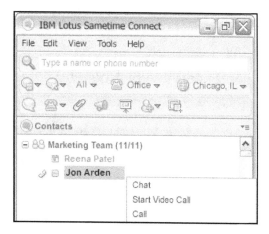

There will also be a phone icon on the action bar to allow you to make phone calls, invite others to a call, or to start a video call.

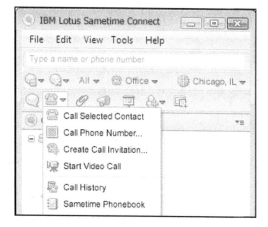

With SUT installed, you have a number of features available to you, including the following:

- Availability and new telephony presence indicators
- Click to call another computer using VoIP
- Click to call another phone

- Click to create a conference call
- Use of the Sametime "softphone" (software that works with your computer, microphone, and headset to make it act like a phone)
- Ability to mute/un-mute, remove, and add participants to a conference call
- Choose your preferred device or phone number
- Transfer calls from one device to another
- Merge two calls into a single call
- Review your call history and record details of your calls

In order to be able to use SUT, you need to have Sametime Connect client version 8.0.2 or Notes Embedded client version 8.0.2 or later installed. In order to see the version of your Sametime Connect client, click on **Help | About Lotus Sametime** menu option.

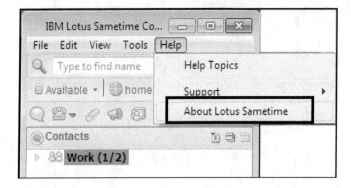

The splash screen that appears will have the version of Sametime on it.

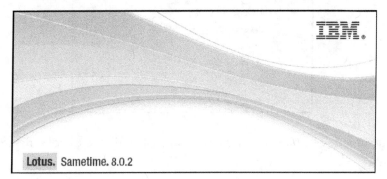

For the Notes Embedded client, confirm your version with your Sametime administrator.

Additionally, the Sametime Connect client and Notes Embedded client require the installation of an add-on to add the SUT components. Your Sametime administrator may have packaged these with your Sametime installation. If you're unsure as to whether or not you require this add-on, check with your Sametime administrator. You can also check for the version of the Lotus Notes Embedded client using the Lotus Sametime Wiki article located at: `http://www-10.lotus.com/ldd/stwiki.nsf/dx/How_to_check_the_version_of_the_Sametime_client_embedded_in_the_Notes_client.`

Using Sametime Unified Telephony features

In *Chapter 5*, we covered how you can make audio and video calls in Sametime by clicking on the telephone icon in the menu bar. Video calls in SUT work much the same way. Your workstation and that of your contact must have additional hardware (webcam, headset, and microphone) for this to work.

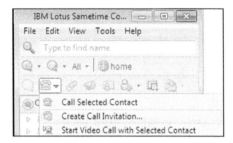

When you're using SUT, there's an additional set of options in the Call drop-down menu. You can call a phone number, which will place a telephone call (through Sametime) to your selected contact. The person receiving the call can determine which device they will use to answer the call.

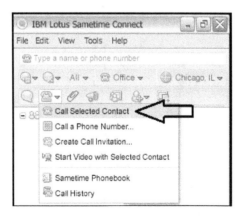

Your Sametime contacts can be reached by phone even if you have multiple Sametime communities. The Sametime server that supports Unified Telephony needs to be included in the community list. Be sure to check with your Sametime administrator if you have questions about this.

When you start to type the phone number in the name/number entry field at the top of the Connect client, Sametime will use a type-ahead feature to list all the numbers that match as you type each character. This is especially helpful if you only remember a portion of the phone number but not all of it.

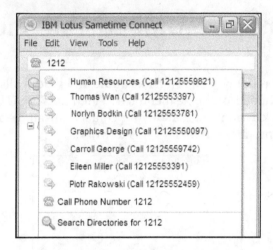

If you'd like to call someone who is not in your contact list, you can place the call by typing out the full number and clicking **Call Phone Number**. If your contact is also a SUT user, when they receive your incoming call, a popup screen will display with your contact information. The pop-up dialog also gives them the option of how to take the call such as answering it on the computer, routing it to another phone, or sending it to voicemail.

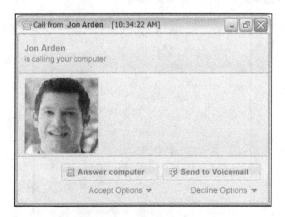

Once your contact accepts the call, they will see a dialog box that remains on the screen while the call is active. To hang up they can click the **Leave Call** icon at the bottom-right corner of the screen.

From the **Actions** menu during the call you can also add in additional callers so that you can have multi-party calls without having to pre-schedule a conference line. You can also drag-and-drop the Sametime contact from the contact list into the call.

It is also very easy to forward the call to someone else. If you click on the phone icon with the upward-facing arrow, the menu for transferring the call to another number or person appears.

Since SUT allows you to work with multiple devices and phone numbers, you can select and set **Preferred Numbers** from your Sametime Preferences. This allows you to enter all your phone numbers with descriptive locations. You can also set the number of seconds that each number or device will ring before it times out and takes an alternative action such as going to voicemail.

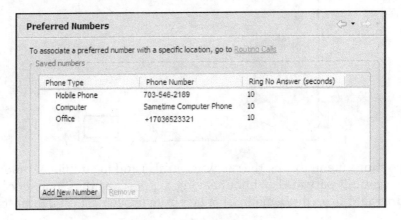

These numbers are shown on your toolbar as the preferred number for your Sametime. This sets the number you want to use to make or receive your calls.

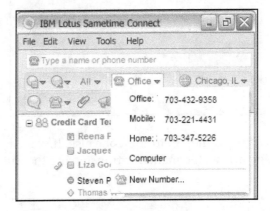

Your Sametime Preferences also have an option for **Routing Calls**. This allows you to set up rules for call routing based on certain conditions and presence awareness status settings. For instance, if you are showing as Away on Sametime, you can define a rule that will route any calls first to your computer in case you're at your desk. Then, if no answer is received by the timeout limit specified for that number, you can have it routed to your mobile phone. You could even have it route to a third number or let the call go to voicemail if you prefer.

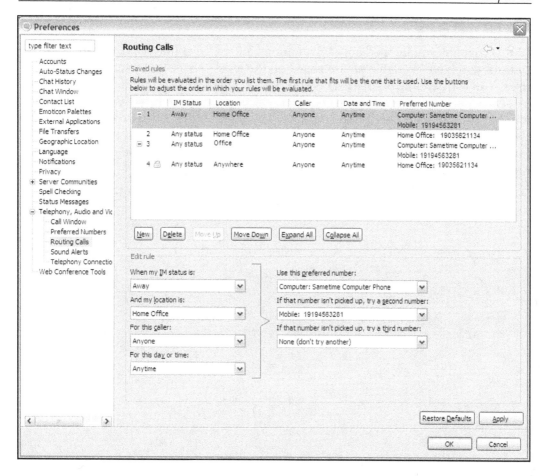

From your Preferences you can also set your Notification options. Choose the **Event**, **Calls**, **Telephony**, **Audio**, and **Video**. For example, if you don't want any notifications for your phone events, clear the **Display incoming notification** selection. This will stop any further notifications of incoming calls.

Getting help

Remember that you can always find help for any of your SUT related tasks. You can select the Help button or the question mark that appears in many of the dialog boxes.

Summary

In this chapter, you learned about Sametime Unified Telephony and the different options you have available to you based on the level of SUT that your organization uses. You learned how to place calls and how to answer calls sent to your computer. You now know how to add people to your call and how to transfer your call to another person or another phone number. This chapter described how you can enter the phone numbers you use so that SUT can recognize them. Finally, you learned how to set up rules within SUT that will route your calls to different numbers based on your current status.

Sametime 8.5 and 8.5.1 New Features

With the release of Sametime 8.5 in December 2009 came the announcement of many new features and improvements to the Sametime product family. Visit the Sametime 8.5 product site for further information at `http://www-01.ibm.com/software/lotus/products/sametime/whatsnew.html`. Sametime 8.5.1 was announced in July 2010, and the new features included in that version can be found at `http://www-01.ibm.com/common/ssi/cgi-bin/ssialia s?subtype=ca&infotype=an&appname=iSource&supplier=897&letternum=ENUS 210-080`. We're going to cover a few of the highlights that may be of use to you as a Sametime user when you migrate to version 8.5 or 8.5.1.

In this appendix you'll learn how to:

- Use the Sametime 8.5 browser-based client
- Identify the new options included in Sametime 8.5 Meeting Rooms
- Add new attendees to your on-going meetings
- Identify the new audio and video features for the Sametime Connect client and Meeting Center
- Get started with the Sametime 8.5 client on the Apple iPhone
- Identify the new client platform options available to Sametime 8.5.1 users
- Understand the changes in chat logging and announcements with Sametime 8.5.1 and how they may affect you

New features in Sametime 8.5

Sametime 8.5 brings many new features to the Sametime client and to online meetings. These include the addition of a browser-based chat client, an Apple iPhone Sametime client, as well as increased functionality for Blackberry and Windows Mobile device clients. Our goal is to introduce you to some of these features so that you may understand how the new features might apply to your environment.

Browser-based client

Since many of you may work in many different locations such as office, home, or laptop, Sametime 8.5 now provides a browser-based chat client. What does this mean? It means that from a web URL you can login to Sametime without having to download any software to your computer. This is a very flexible option for those who work from kiosks or workstations that have no administrator privileges. Simply type in the URL that your Sametime administrator has provided you, click on the Launch Sametime button, and you'll see the new Sametime 8.5 browser client login screen!

You'll notice that the login looks very similar to the Sametime Connect client login. You can set your availability from the login button.

Just like in previous versions of Sametime, your contact list resides on the server, so even when you login with the browser client, your Sametime contact list will be available to you. You can invite others to your chats and Meeting Rooms, modify your privacy settings, and send announcements. The availability settings for yourself and others have not changed.

The announcement of Sametime 8.5.1 included the availability of additional support for new client platforms including Blackberry 5.0 devices, Windows Mobile 6.5 devices, Windows 7.0, Macintosh 10.6, and Linux (SUSE Linux Enterprise Desktop (SLED), Ubuntu, and Red Hat Enterprise Desktop (RHED)).

Sametime 8.5 meetings

Sametime 8.5 packed lots of new functionality into the use of online meetings. Sametime meetings no longer require any sort of applet to be downloaded for the meeting to take place. The meeting is either run from the new rich meeting client installed as part of the Sametime client or run from a browser with no additional programs to install. Also, Sametime 8.5 meetings no longer require a reservation to set up. They occur in Meeting Rooms that permanently exist, just as if they were a physical conference room. They are also persistent, in that they can retain the content of previous visits to that particular meeting unless you choose to clear that content out. And you as an individual can have multiple Meeting Rooms based on different characteristics such as different projects or different project teams.

Meetings are now integrated as a separate toolbar in the Sametime Connect client. The Meeting bar gives you the option of reviewing your Meeting Room list.

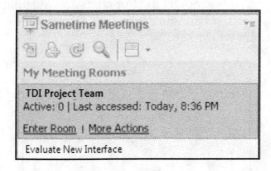

Remember how you had to sign into a meeting in Sametime 8.0.2? Sametime 8.5 has made it much easier. You simply join a meeting with a single click. Inviting others to your meetings is also easier. You may drag-and-drop their names from your contact list or send them a meeting invite. The invite will appear as a pop up on their Sametime client if they are using Sametime 8.5 — which they can join or decline — or as a Sametime 8.0.2 user they will see a pop up with the URL of the meeting which they can only attend through a browser.

Meeting materials such as slides, audio, or visual presentations can be uploaded through drag-and-drop from your desktop as well.

Sametime 8.5 also includes changes in the audio and video components. This now includes a standards-based infrastructure that allows integration with existing third-party audio and video conferencing systems.

iPhone and Sametime 8.5

The Apple iPhone now has its very own browser-based Sametime Connect client in the Sametime 8.5 world. It looks very much like every other Sametime interface except that it has been developed so that you as an iPhone user can take advantage of the touch screen.

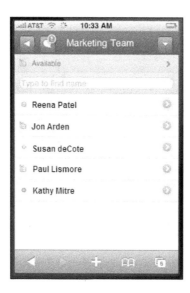

As with most iPhone applications, this application will also work on your Apple iPad.

Summary

In this chapter, you learned about the new features of Sametime 8.5 and how they might affect you as a Sametime user. You learned that Sametime 8.5.1 introduced some new client platforms. You learned about how Sametime 8.5 uses the web browser more effectively as well as how much easier it is to create meetings and invite people. Finally, you learned that iPhone users have their own Sametime client much like users of other mobile devices. As we go to press we're sure that many new additional features and clients for Sametime will be released in the near future.

B
Using Sametime in Chat-Enabled Applications

Sametime interfaces are not only used with the Sametime Connect client or Meeting Center. You can also use Sametime in Lotus Quickr — the web-based team collaboration software, Lotus Connections — social software, custom built applications, and Microsoft products. We'll introduce you to Sametime operability available in each of these areas.

In this chapter, you'll learn how to:

- Determine if a Lotus Quickr site is enabled for Sametime
- Chat with others who are logged into a Lotus Quickr site
- Recognize Sametime integration in Lotus Connections
- Recognize Sametime integration in the Notes client
- Recognize Sametime integration in a Notes-based application
- Find information about Sametime integration with Microsoft Outlook, Office, and SharePoint

Lotus Quickr

Lotus Quickr is team collaboration software that includes the ability to create websites for team projects, wikis, blogs, and libraries for your team, company, or organization. A Quickr site has built-in security and includes team calendars and discussion templates. Your Sametime administrator can work with your company or organization's Quickr administrator to "Sametime-enable" your Quickr environment. How can you as a user recognize that your Quickr site is enabled for Sametime? When you login to Quickr, you'll notice that the Sametime availability icon displays by your name.

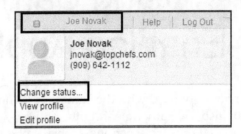

From here you can change your Sametime status, view your profile and edit your profile.

To begin chatting with those individuals who are logged into the Quickr site, click the **Chat** in the **Place Tools** section in the Table of Contents of your Quickr site.

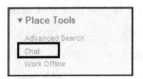

The **Members Online** dialog box will appear. Double-click on the name of the person with whom you want to chat.

You can also set up a multi-way chat with several members. You can invite all online members to a chat by right-clicking on a user's name and then clicking **Invite All**. If you only want to include certain individuals, select their name and hold down the *Shift* or *Ctrl* key, then right-click on the selected names.

Sametime and Lotus Connections

Lotus Connections is a social software application that allows you to interact with individuals and teams in your company or organization through blogs, wikis, communities, and activities. The Lotus Connections administrator can configure Connections to enable Sametime awareness. As a Connections user, you may see awareness enabled in Connections Activities, Profiles, and Communities. Check with your Lotus Connections administrator if you have any questions about using Sametime.

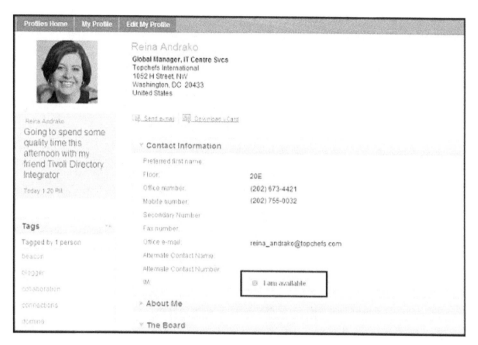

Sametime and custom applications

If you use Lotus Notes for e-mail, you can launch many of the Sametime functions without even leaving the e-mail that you're currently reading. The Sametime presence awareness icon shows up next to the name of someone if they're currently active on Sametime.

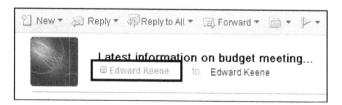

If your Sametime preferences are configured to display, **Show business card when you hover over a contact's name**, when you move your mouse over the icon, the person's business card information will appear so that you can get their location, phone numbers, and other information they share with others.

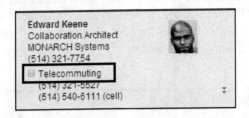

Right-clicking the icon brings up the Sametime menu of options and from there you can start chats, invite the person to an instant meeting, or invoke any other Sametime function that will help you communicate more effectively.

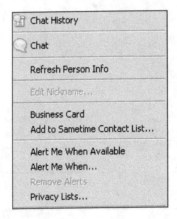

This same type of Sametime integration can also be part of any custom Lotus Notes application. Forms that have name fields can be set to show online presence when the developer builds the application. In the following example, we have a Notes journal database that is used to store presentation documents. You'll notice that the Sametime awareness icon is next to the Submitter's name in both the Entry line and in the actual document itself. Because that icon is there, you can click on it to begin chatting with the individual or determine their online status. In this case, the author of the document is online.

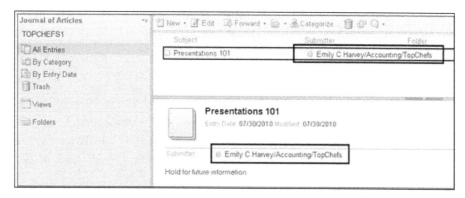

Notes developers can "enable" Sametime features in Notes applications very easily by checking the option, **Show online status** on a Name field, and this option will automatically activate the Sametime integration.

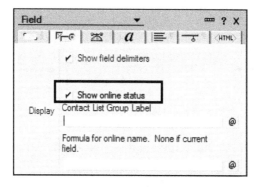

If you don't see that type of Sametime integration in your Notes application, ask your development staff if it is possible for them to make this type of enhancement to the application.

Sametime and Microsoft products

Lotus Sametime can even integrate into your Microsoft Office, Microsoft Outlook, and Microsoft SharePoint applications. When names appear in those applications, you can click on the presence icons to start chats and instant meetings. You install Sametime Microsoft Office Integration as a plug-in to your Sametime Connect client. We're not going to discuss the installation in detail, but this link will provide you with an overview: `http://publib.boulder.ibm.com/infocenter/sametime/v8r0/index.jsp?topic=/com.ibm.help.sametime.802.doc/Standard/st_inst_optionalfeatures_t.html`. If you're not sure you have the Microsoft Office Integration plug-in installed, contact your Sametime administrator for assistance.

When Microsoft Office Integration is installed, if you're using Microsoft Outlook, for example, you see a Sametime toolbar added to your Outlook toolbar. It provides you with options to:

- Open your Sametime contact list
- Search for your Sametime contacts and the Sametime address book
- Start a Sametime chat, telephone call, video call, or voice chat, with a person in your contact list, or the person in your e-mail list, if they are accessible through Sametime
- Begin a Sametime Meeting

This figure shows what your Microsoft Outlook toolbar might look like after the plugin has been installed, and you've logged in through the Sametime Connect client:

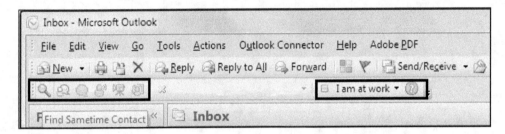

Notice that it also displays your online status, just as the Sametime Connect client or Sametime Embedded client does.

The toolbar also works from Outlook Calendar. As with other Sametime clients, you can modify your online status:

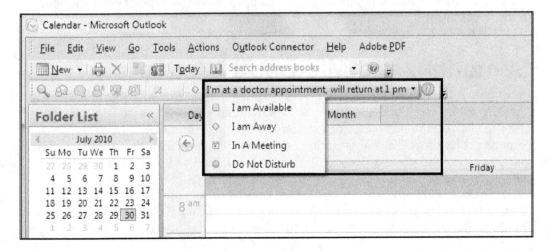

Sametime integration also works with other Microsoft Office products. For example, Sametime adds a separate toolbar command to the **Add-Ins** tab of Microsoft Word.

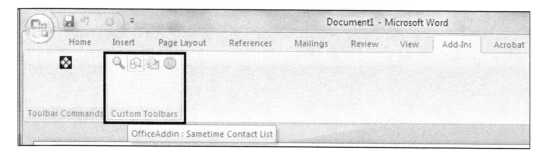

As with other Sametime products, if you need help while using Sametime there is generally a help button. In this case if you click the question mark, the help dialog relating to Sametime and Microsoft Office integration will display.

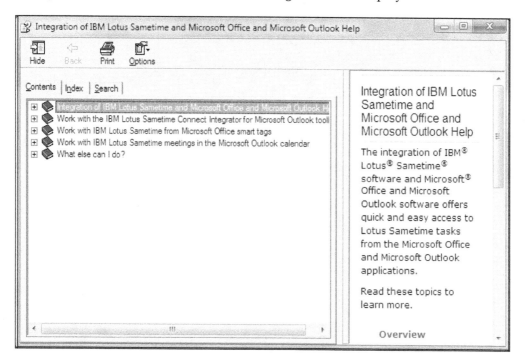

This link gives you an overview of the different types of integration you can expect between Sametime and Microsoft: `http://www-01.ibm.com/software/lotus /products/sametime/appintegration.html`

Summary

In this Appendix, you learned how Lotus Sametime integrates with Lotus Quickr, Lotus Connections, Lotus Notes applications, and Microsoft software. You also learned how to determine if Sametime integration is present in the application you're using.

C
Additional Sametime Resources

In addition to the information you've read in this book, you can find a wealth of information and resources online. IBM and the Lotus Sametime community are continuously publishing and sharing new information and user aids. In the next few pages, we will point you to some Sametime resources that we've found useful, informative, and even entertaining.

Sametime basics

IBM's Sametime product home page:

```
http://www-01.ibm.com/software/lotus/sametime/
```

IBM has a Sametime wiki site that is constantly being updated by the Sametime community. This is a great reference point for the user and contains technical information related to Sametime:

```
http://www-10.lotus.com/ldd/stwiki.nsf
```

A list of keyboard shortcuts for Sametime running on Windows:

```
http://publib.boulder.ibm.com/infocenter/sametime/v8r0/index.
jsp?topic=/com.ibm.help.sametime.801.doc/Connect/r_st8_uim_
accessibility.html
```

The full online version of the Sametime Help files:

```
http://publib.boulder.ibm.com/infocenter/sametime/v8r0/index.jsp
```

If you'd like to try out Sametime in your own personal "sandbox", you can get a 60-day trial edition of Sametime Standard:

```
http://www.ibm.com/developerworks/downloads/ls/lst/
```

This page has demos of Sametime 8, Sametime Advanced, Frequently Asked Questions, and a handy reference card to help you remember the essentials:

```
http://www-10.lotus.com/ldd/stwiki.nsf/dx/Getting_started_Lotus_
Sametime_8
```

Sametime client feature how-to's

Annotating a screen capture is a powerful feature used to convey information to your chat partner. Here's a demo of how you can do that:

```
http://www-10.lotus.com/ldd/stwiki.nsf/dx/Demo_Annotating_a_screen_
capture_%288.0%29
```

If you want to keep all your chat windows in a single tabbed interface, this demo will walk you through how to do it:

```
http://www-10.lotus.com/ldd/stwiki.nsf/dx/Demo_Consolidating_chats_
into_a_single_tabbed_window_%288.0%29
```

If you have your Sametime client set up to save chat history, you can quickly find transcripts of all your chats. This demo shows you how:

```
http://www-10.lotus.com/ldd/stwiki.nsf/dx/Demo_Opening_a_saved_chat_
transcript
```

Sharing your screen with others is one of the most powerful features of Sametime. Here is a demo to show you how it is done:

```
http://www-10.lotus.com/ldd/stwiki.nsf/dx/Demo_
```

Sametime Advanced

Sametime Advanced and features specific to that version of Sametime such as Broadcast Chat can be seen in the demo here:

```
http://www-10.lotus.com/ldd/stwiki.nsf/dx/Getting_started_Lotus_
Sametime_Advanced_8
```

Sametime Advanced reference cards can be found here:

```
http://www-10.lotus.com/ldd/stwiki.nsf/dx/Lotus_Sametime_Reference_
Cards
```

Creating a Skill Tap FAQ is a great way to capture your group's knowledge for others. Watch this demo on how it is done:

```
http://www-10.lotus.com/ldd/stwiki.nsf/dx/Demo_Creating_and_rating_a_
Skill_Tap_FAQ_%288.0_Advanced%29
```

If you're still unsure as to why Sametime Advanced would be a useful addition to your environment, this article highlights the benefits:

```
http://www.ibm.com/developerworks/lotus/library/sametime8-advanced/
```

Sametime Unified Telephony

Sametime Unified Telephony product information can be found here:

```
http://www-01.ibm.com/software/lotus/products/sametime/
unifiedtelephony/
```

For reference cards, demos, and online seminars about Sametime Unified Telephony:

```
http://www-10.lotus.com/ldd/stwiki.nsf/dx/Lotus_Sametime_Telephony_8_
Resources_for_users
```

If you're not scared off by acronyms, protocols, and standards, see this site for detailed technical information about Sametime Unified Telephony:

```
http://download.boulder.ibm.com/ibmdl/pub/software/dw/lotus/SUTfinal.
pdf
```

Sametime 8.5 information

Sametime 8.5 product information can be found here:

```
http://www-01.ibm.com/software/lotus/products/sametime/whatsnew.html
```

For Sametime 8.5 demos and reference cards see the Sametime wiki:

```
http://www-10.lotus.com/ldd/stwiki.nsf/dx/Getting_started_Lotus_
Sametime_8.5
```

A very useful document about integrating Sametime 8.5 with Microsoft products:

```
http://publib.boulder.ibm.com/infocenter/sametime/v8r5/topic/com.ibm.
help.sametime.v85.doc/st_oi-pdf.pdf
```

Help documentation for all the various Sametime 8.5 clients can be found here:

```
http://publib.boulder.ibm.com/infocenter/sametime/v8r5/index.
jsp?topic=/com.ibm.help.sametime.user.doc/mobile/welcome.html
```

Miscellaneous Sametime information

Check out the Sametime blog for updates and inside information about using Sametime:

```
https://www-950.ibm.com/blogs/SametimeBlog/?lang=en_us
```

Sometimes it's easier to ask a question of someone than to dig through countless pages of documentation that may be confusing or unclear. While the Lotus Sametime Forum is more geared towards development and administration, you may find fellow users who have had the same issues you have (and have answers):

```
http://www-10.lotus.com/ldd/stforum.nsf
```

If you're running Quickr and Sametime and having problems getting the two software packages to integrate, this document can help you in your troubleshooting efforts:

```
http://www.ibm.com/developerworks/lotus/documentation/d-ls-
stquickrtroubleshoot/
```

You may want to develop applications that use Sametime as a core function. A good resource for those efforts is at:

```
http://www-10.lotus.com/ldd/stwiki.nsf/dx/learning_stadv_devs.htm
```

Sametime can integrate with Lotus Connections, IBM's social networking product. In this link, you see how a broadcast chat can be linked to a Connections forum:

```
http://www-10.lotus.com/ldd/stwiki.nsf/dx/demo-of-sametime-advanced-
broadcast-chat-working-with-lotus-connections
```

Check out these videos from Epilio (`http://www.epilio.com`) for step-by-step instructions on installing plug-ins for the Sametime 8 client and the Notes 8.x embedded client:

`http://www.youtube.com/watch?v=_HAY2b5YwLg`

`http://www.youtube.com/watch?v=OqotsM56mFM`

Sametime integrates with the following Microsoft products: Outlook, Office, and SharePoint. Refer to this site for general information:

`http://www-10.lotus.com/ldd/stwiki.nsf/dx/test-infrastructures-sametime-8.0.2-microsoft-office-integration-with-ipv6`

Installing patches for Sametime Connect and Microsoft Integration:

`http://www-01.ibm.com/support/docview.wss?rss=477&uid=swg21307607`

IBM developerWorks is a site that contains articles, tutorials, and various other resources geared towards the technical community. As a developer, you'll learn how to extend Sametime to make it even more integral to your environment. As a user, you'll get ideas on how your organization can leverage Sametime beyond the "out-of-the-box" experience:

`http://www.ibm.com/developerworks/lotus/products/instantmessaging`

If you're a developer and want to begin developing applications or plug-ins specifically for Sametime, see the Sametime development toolkit which can be downloaded free:

`http://www14.software.ibm.com/webapp/download/nochargesearch.jsp?q0=&k=ALL&S_TACT=104CBW71&status=Active&b=Lotus&sr=1&q=sametime+sdk&ibm-search=Search`

Sametime plug-ins from third-party vendors can add more functionality to your Sametime client. Here's a list of available Sametime plug-ins from the IBM Greenhouse:

`https://greenhouse.lotus.com/catalog/home_full.xsp?fProduct=Lotus%20Sametime`

The Multimedia Library for Lotus Software offering is an IBM offering that gives you access to hundreds of video tutorials that focus on small, discrete tasks such as adding contacts or sharing your screen. A cost-effective way to train your users on Sametime:

`http://www-01.ibm.com/software/lotus/training/multimedialibrary.html`

The "Official" Sametime song

If you need a break from all the "seriousness" of Sametime, go listen to the Sametime Song!

```
http://www-10.lotus.com/ldd/stwiki.nsf/dx/Sametime_Song
```

Index

C

contact list option 19, 40
contact nicknames 56-58
contacts, iNotes Sametime
  adding 126
  managing 127, 128
contacts, Sametime
  about 20
  Add Contact dialog box 59
  Add Contacts option 20
  adding 49, 126
  adding, from inbox 51
  adding, ways 50, 51
  Add Sametime Contact dialog box 50, 51
  Add tab 22
  Add to Sametime Contact List option 51
  Add to Sametime Contact List tab 22
  and business card information 63-65
  contact list, sorting 61
  contact lists between different locations,
      merging 62
  Contacts A-Z 128
  Day-At-A-Glance appointments 125
  displaying, in sidebar 125, 126
  exporting 53
  Groups A-Z 128
  group, sorting 61
  importing 53
  list 48
  Lookup button 50
  Lookup tab 21
  managing 48, 127, 128
  managing, with contact groups 59
  new group, creating 59
  New Sametime Contact 49
  nicknames 56, 57, 58
  online contacts, displaying 54
  Online Only 128
  preferences, setting 54
  public group 60
  Remove from Sametime Contact List option
      53
  removing 53
  Sidebar Panels 125
  Show Sametime Contact List 126
  type ahead feature 48
  Work contact category 20
Contacts A-Z 128

custom applications
  and Sametime 245-247
customized status messages, Sametime
      Mobile client preferences
  setting up 141, 142

D

date stamps
  about 81
  Display Datestamps in Chat Transcript
      option 81
  Display Timestamps in Chat Transcript
      option 81
  Sametime | Chat Window 81
  setting 81
Day-At-A-Glance appointments 125
demos, Sametime 8.5
  URL 253
directory types
  about 56
  Browse for Name tab 56
  Domino versus LDAP 117, 118
Disable Chat Transcript button 85
Display Datestamps in Chat Transcript
      option 81
display preferences, Sametime Mobile
      client preferences
  changing 140
Display Timestamps in Chat Transcript
      option 81
Domino Address Book 24
Domino directory
  versus LDAP directory 117, 118
Do not disturb, status 24

E

embedded Sametime client 13, 14
emoticon palettes option 20, 40
emoticons
  about 95
  Add to emoticon palette 98
  Edit... button 96
  Export Palette dialog 98
  options 97
  Restore Defaults button 98
emotion icons. *See* emoticons

Enable Instant messaging option 121
Epilio
  videos, URL 255
  website, URL 42
Essentials tab 155
Export Palette dialog 98
external applications option 40
external Sametime communities
  about 110
  Add New Server Community 110
  Remove button 112
  Sametime Contacts bar 110
  Server Communities option 111

F

files
  sending 87
  sending, icon 79
  transfer, cancelling 88
  transfer, limit 89
  types 89
file transfers option 20, 40
file types, whiteboarding
  supported 184, 185
foreground text color
  changing 78
Frequently Asked Questions, URL 252

G

geographic location option 20, 40
Google option 114
graphics
  sending 89
group chat
  about 73, 171
  Name field 74
  Send button 74
  starting 73, 74
groups, Sametime Mobile
  managing from 144, 145
Groups A-Z 128

H

Help 130
help, Sametime Advanced 224, 225

help, Sametime Meeting Center 198
Help | Help Topics, meeting 173
help feature, Sametime Mobile 146
Help files
  URL 251
Host server 15
hyperlink 79

I

I'm in a meeting, status 23
I am available, status 23
I am away, status 23
IBM's Sametime product home page
  URL 251
IBM developerWorks 255
IBM Lotus Sametime 7
icons
  background text color 78
  bold text 79
  chat encrypted 79
  check spelling 79
  file sending 79
  foreground text color 78
  hyperlink 79
  insert emoticon 79
  italics text 79
  screen capture 79
  text properties 78
  text setting dialog box 78
  text size 78, 79
  underlined text 79
inbox
  contacts, adding from 51
iNotes Sametime
  Add Tools icon 124
  Add to Sametime Contact List 123
  Add to the Sametime Contact List... 123
  chatting from 122-125
  chat window 124
  Chat with 123
  Chat with... option 123
  contacts, adding 126
  contacts, manging 128
  Help 130
  instant messaging, enabling 121, 122
  Sametime, using 120

privacy option 20, 40
privacy settings 69, 71

Q

Quickr
  and Sametime, URL 254
quick responses, Sametime Mobile client
    139
Quickr site 244

R

reference cards, Sametime 8.5
  URL 253
Remember Password checkbox 16
Remove button 112
Remove from Sametime Contact List option
    53
Replay the Meeting button 194
Restore Default button 54
Restrict the meeting to the following users
    option 156
rich text style 80, 81

S

Sametime
  about 7
  accessibility option 19
  advanced and features specific, URL 252
  advanced level 11
  Advanced reference cards, URL 253
  alerts 72
  and custom applications 245-247
  and iNotes 120
  and Lotus Connections 245
  and Microsoft products 247-249
  and Quickr, URL 254
  announcements, sending 91, 92
  article, URL 253
  audio option 20
  audio services 98, 99
  auto-status changes option 19
  Automatically log in checkbox 16
  blog for updates, URL 254
  business card information 63-65
  chat, starting with contact 24

chat history 82
chat history option 19
chat messages, spell-checking 85, 86
chat tool bar, 78, 79
chat tool bar, icons 78, 79
chat transcript finding, URL 252
chat window option 19
clients, types 10
Connect 10
connecting to 15, 16
Connectivity button 17
contact, adding 20, 126
contacts, displaying in sidebar 125, 126
contact list option 19
contact nicknames 56-58
contacts 20
contacts, adding 49, 50
contacts, exporting 53, 54
contacts, importing 53, 54
contacts, managing 48, 127, 128
contacts, removing 53
Contacts A-Z 128
date stamps 81
development toolkit, URL 255
directory types 56
Embedded Client 10
emoticons 95, 96
emoticon palettes option 20
entry level 11
external Sametime communities, connecting
  to 110-113
features 18
file transfers option 20
files, sending 87-89
for Lotus iNotes 10
Frequently Asked Questions, URL 252
geographic location option 20
geographic locations 223
graphics, sending 89
Groups A-Z 128
Help 130
help files, online version URL 251
Host server 15
IBM's Sametime product home page,
  URL 251
importance 9
in Lotus Quickr 243, 244

Thank you for buying
IBM Lotus Sametime 8 Essentials – A User's Guide

About Packt Publishing

Packt, pronounced 'packed', published its first book "Mastering phpMyAdmin for Effective MySQL Management" in April 2004 and subsequently continued to specialize in publishing highly focused books on specific technologies and solutions.

Our books and publications share the experiences of your fellow IT professionals in adapting and customizing today's systems, applications, and frameworks. Our solution based books give you the knowledge and power to customize the software and technologies you're using to get the job done. Packt books are more specific and less general than the IT books you have seen in the past. Our unique business model allows us to bring you more focused information, giving you more of what you need to know, and less of what you don't.

Packt is a modern, yet unique publishing company, which focuses on producing quality, cutting-edge books for communities of developers, administrators, and newbies alike. For more information, please visit our website: www.packtpub.com.

About Packt Enterprise

In 2010, Packt launched two new brands, Packt Enterprise and Packt Open Source, in order to continue its focus on specialization. This book is part of the Packt Enterprise brand, home to books published on enterprise software – software created by major vendors, including (but not limited to) IBM, Microsoft and Oracle, often for use in other corporations. Its titles will offer information relevant to a range of users of this software, including administrators, developers, architects, and end users.

Writing for Packt

We welcome all inquiries from people who are interested in authoring. Book proposals should be sent to author@packtpub.com. If your book idea is still at an early stage and you would like to discuss it first before writing a formal book proposal, contact us; one of our commissioning editors will get in touch with you.

We're not just looking for published authors; if you have strong technical skills but no writing experience, our experienced editors can help you develop a writing career, or simply get some additional reward for your expertise..

IBM Lotus Notes and Domino 8.5.1

ISBN: 978-1-847199-28-7   Paperback: 336 pages

Upgrade your system and embrace the exciting new features of the Lotus Notes and Domino 8.5.1 platform

1. Upgrade to the latest version of Lotus Notes and Domino

2. Understand the new features and put them to work in your business

3. Thoroughly covers Domino Attachment Object Service (DAOS), Domino Configuration Tuner (DCT), and iNotes

IBM Lotus Notes 8.5 User Guide

ISBN: 978-1-849680-20-2   Paperback: 296 pages

A practical hands-on user guide with time saving tips and comprehensive instructions for using Lotus Notes effectively and efficiently

1. Understand and master the features of Lotus Notes and put them to work in your business quickly

2. Contains comprehensive coverage of new Lotus Notes 8.5 features

3. Includes easy-to-follow real-world examples with plenty of screenshots to clearly demonstrate how to get the most out of Lotus Notes

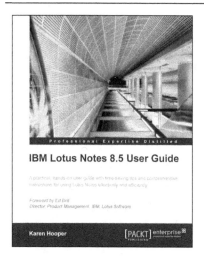

Please check **www.PacktPub.com** for information on our titles